Horseback Riding Trails

of

Southern California

Volume I

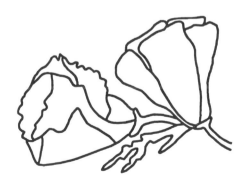

HORSEBACK RIDING TRAILS
OF
SOUTHERN CALIFORNIA

VOLUME I

BY
PAULETTE MOUCHET

CROWN VALLEY PRESS
P.O. Box 336
ACTON, CA 93510
(805) 269-1525

IMPORTANT LEGAL NOTICE AND DISCLAIMER

Horseback riding is a potentially dangerous sport, and the rider or user of this book accepts a number of risks. While substantial effort has been made to provide accurate information, this guidebook may inadvertently contain errors and omissions. The maps in this book are for locator reference only. They are not to be used for navigation and are intended to complement large-scale topo maps. Your mileages may vary from those given in this book.

The author, contributors, publisher, and distributors accept no liability for any errors or omissions in this book, or for any injuries or losses incurred from using this book.

Library of Congress Cataloging-in-Publication Data
Mouchet, Paulette
      Horseback Riding Trails of Southern California Volume I/Paulette Mouchet.
      v. :ill. ; 128 p.; 21.6 cm.
      Includes bibliographical references and index.
      ISBN 0-9647945-0-0
      1. Trails -- California -- Guide-books. 2. California, Southern -- Description and travel -- Guide-books. 3. California -- Description and travel -- 1981- -- Guide-books. 4. Horses -- Miscellanea. 5. Horse sports. I. Title
SF309.256.C2 M68 1995
                                     95-92581
                                       CIP

ACKNOWLEDGMENTS

As with any book of this nature, turning the dream into reality takes more than jeans in the saddle and fingers at the computer keyboard. Without the ideas, suggestions, enthusiasm, and support of the wonderful folks I met along the trail, I would have given up long ago and missed out on a great adventure in doing so.

I'd like to thank my husband who has championed my writing from the day I announced, "I'm going to write a novel." He is my faithful riding companion, chauffeur, computer guru, camera wizard, and all-around the most wonderful man a woman could have.

Special thanks to my adopted mother, Pat, for her generosity and for encouraging me to follow my dreams.

Thanks to Jennifer and Rick Fuller for their enthusiasm, for exploring new trails, and for sharing some great camping meals.

Thanks to Bruce and Laurie Berger for squeezing me into their jammed schedules. Thanks for sharing trails with me, bailing me out when the truck broke down, and putting up with my crabbiness when I got heat stroke.

Thanks to Milt and Maxine Mc Auley for answering a zillion questions about the publishing industry. Thanks to Helen Eagan and Jan Hill for sharing their experiences with publishing their trail guide for the Denver area. Thanks to Wayne Marteney, DVM, for reviewing the "First-aid Kit." Thanks to Kay at Thomson-Shore for being a friend. Thanks to Sharon at PeopleSpeak for her eagle eye, great humor, and marketing savvy. Thanks to the folks at SVC for their enthusiasm and encouragement. And thanks to Holly Carson, editor of the *Equestrian Trails* magazine, and the many folks in E.T.I. who shared trail information.

Finally, thanks to our four-footed friends, Sam and Centella, who faithfully carried my husband and me on the many miles of trails we explored.

ABOUT THE AUTHOR

Paulette Mouchet has owned horses for more than twenty-five years and enjoys riding and exploring new trails with her husband. She writes both fiction and nonfiction, and her work has been published in magazines and newspapers.

TABLE OF CONTENTS

TRAILS BY AREA

LIST OF MAPS

PREFACE

Thank you for purchasing Volume I of *Horseback Riding Trails of Southern California*.

When my husband and I bought our first horse trailer, we could not find a practical guide to riding trails. Being new to trailering, we didn't want to hook up and drive someplace when we didn't know exactly where that "someplace" was, or if there would be trailer parking when we got there, or if our horses could handle the trails. As we collected information for ourselves, it seemed obvious and appropriate that we should make it available to anyone who wanted to experience new trails.

My goal is to provide accurate directions and detailed information about facilities so that you can get to a location, park, and enjoy exploring the trails yourself. Many sites have overnight facilities and I have indicated them. Horseback riding is an activity that the entire family can enjoy, and I hope you have as much fun as my husband and I did.

From the time I began this project until now, trail conditions may have changed, new trails may have been developed, and others may have been lost due to neglect. If you have comments or suggestions, or would like to contribute to Volume II, please write to me in care of Crown Valley Press at the address listed below. I would like to hear from you.

Good riding!

ATTENTION EQUINE ORGANIZATIONS AND PRODUCT AND SERVICE PROVIDERS: Quantity discounts are available on bulk purchases of this book. For information contact Crown Valley Press, P.O. Box 336, Acton CA 93510, (805) 269-1525.

SAFETY FIRST

Safety Tips

Plan ahead. Keep your cool. Carry first-aid supplies.

Newcomers and seasoned riders alike should be aware that horseback riding can be a dangerous sport. Accidents can happen in the blink of an eye, sometimes in remote locations. The goal of this book is for you and your horse to have an enjoyable ride.   Don't let that be ruined by an avoidable mishap. Please take a few minutes to read the following safety tips.

• Condition yourself and your horse.   Too many accidents occur because the horse and/or rider just aren't up to the job. A tired horse may stumble and throw the rider. A tired rider may take unnecessary risks.

• Check and maintain your equipment.   This includes your trailer as well as your tack. Follow your trailer manu-facturer's maintenance schedule for wheel bearings and brakes.

• Don't ride alone. If you or your horse is hurt, your buddy can go for help.

• Carry a halter, pocket knife, wire cutters, and water. See page 111 for a list of general supplies to bring.

- Wear protective clothing. Consider protective head gear. Hard hats are available in western hat styles. See page 118 for a list of suppliers.

- Observe good trail manners. See page 18 for guidelines. Don't crowd each other, especially going up and down hills, and don't race.

- Carry a basic first-aid kit for both you and your horse. See page 113 for a suggested first-aid kit. Check your kit every 6 months and replace items that are expired or depleted.

- Know your limits and stick to them. Don't let others pressure you into riding farther or faster than you or your horse are conditioned for.

   A CB radio or cellular phone in your towing vehicle may be helpful, and you might consider taking a CPR and basic first-aid course. For classes in your area, contact your local Red Cross.

   Ultimately, be prepared. Knowledge of first aid and basic safety rules will give you self-confidence and enable you to more thoroughly enjoy your ride.

Mountain Lions

Many of the trails listed in this guide traverse mountain lion country. To see a lion in its native habitat can be a thrilling part of your ride. However, mountain lions, also known as cougars, panthers, or pumas, are wild predators and deserve your utmost respect. An adult male averages 6 feet long and can weigh 165 pounds. The head is relatively small with a black spot above each eye, the feet oversized, and the tail thick and nearly as long as the body. With growing urban expansion into wildlife habitat, an increased number of human/lion encounters have been reported. Always stay alert when riding. You are a visitor in their territory.

If you see a mountain lion:

- Do not approach.
- Make yourself look as big as possible and slowly back away.
- Do not run or make sudden moves.
- Do not dismount or crouch down.
- Report any sightings to the appropriate agency.
- Keep your dog on a leash. Better yet, leave him home.

Rattlesnakes

Rattlesnakes are a common southern California inhabitant ranging from the coast to the higher mountain elevations. Of the six species found, the Western rattlesnake (*Crotalus viridis*) is the most widespread. While any rattlesnake bite is serious, the Mojave rattler (*C. scutulatus*) bite is the most deadly. Your best defense against a snakebite is to stay alert and give a wide berth to any snake you encounter. Most snakes will leave you alone if you give them the chance.

According to Glenn R. Stewart, Ph.D., bites from most rattlesnakes are not a life or death matter. Between 20 and 30% of rattlesnake bites introduce no venom at all, and most bites introduce venom only into the subcutaneous tissue.

The action of venom includes direct destruction of tissues and blood vessels, which causes much swelling and pain at the site of the bite.   Venom of the Mojave rattlesnake impairs nerve and neuro-muscular function, and the bite produces little swelling or pain.

Early symptoms of mild to moderate envenomation from most rattlesnake bites include mild swelling or discoloration and mild to moderate pain at the site of the bite.   These symptoms are often accompanied by tingling, rapid pulse, weakness, dimness of vision, nausea, vomiting, and shortness of breath.

Symptoms of severe envenomation include rapid swelling and numbness followed by intense pain at the site of the bite.   Other symptoms include pinpoint pupils, twitching, slurred speech, shock, convulsions, paralysis, unconsciousness, and failure of breathing and pulse.

Snake Identification

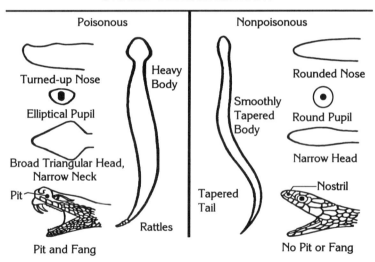

The definitive treatment is antivenin (purified serum, usually from horses, containing antibodies to neutralize the venom components).   If antivenin is administered within 60 minutes of the bite, the chances of death from most bites are quite small.   A victim in a truly remote area (more than 1 hour from medical treatment) may benefit from the use of powerful suction (e.g., the "Sawyer Extractor") at the bite site.   Antivenin can be administered in the field by untrained persons.   You may want to consult with your family physician regarding the use of antivenin and/or the Sawyer Extractor.

If you are bitten:

- Remain calm.
- Remove rings, bracelets, watchbands, etc., from all extremities.
- Immobilize the bitten part with a sling or splint.
- Keep bitten part below heart level and minimize physical activity.
- Seek medical treatment as soon as possible.
- Have your riding partner try to capture and kill the snake so it may be presented for positive identification when you receive medical treatment.

Ticks

With Lyme disease on the rise in California and the nation, you should take precautions against ticks, the most common known vector of the disease. Caused by the corkscrew-shaped bacteria *Borrelia burgdorferi*, Lyme disease affects both humans and animals.

Some signs of the disease in humans:

- Rash with large, distinctive circular lesions first seen around the area of the bite (only 50-60% of patients have this rash); rash may come and go
- Malaise
- Fever
- Muscle aches
- Swollen lymph glands

This list is not complete. Consult your physician for more information.

Deer ticks are the most common carrier of Lyme disease. They are very small, approximately 1/16-inch wide, and orange-brown with a black spot near the head.

After any ride, check yourself thoroughly and immediately seek medical attention if you have been bitten and notice any of the symptoms listed.   If not treated early, the disease can affect heart function and cause arthritis of the major joints.

Wear long sleeves and pants when riding, and use an insect repellent designed for ticks.   Apply a tick-killing fly spray to your horse and routinely check all animals for ticks.

If you find an imbedded tick, touch it with a heated knife.   The tick will "back out" allowing you to grab and squash it with tweezers or a hemostat.   Thoroughly wash the bite area, your hands, and all removal equipment.

Poison Oak

For most people, an encounter with poison oak results in an inflamed, red, scaly, and extremely itchy rash that heals in approximately 2 to 3 weeks.   Occasionally, a person is hyperallergic and will develop severe dermatitis and possibly anaphylactic shock if he or she does not receive immediate medical treatment.   The rash is spread by scratching.   Oral antihistamine and over-the-counter hydrocortisone cream will help control the itching.   In more severe cases, oral steroids may be prescribed by your family doctor.

Take the time to recognize this plant in all its disguises, and then avoid it! Poison oak is widespread throughout the areas listed in this guide. Normally an erect shrub 4 to 8 feet tall, it sometimes twines along the trunks of trees. The leaves are bright green in the spring, turn orange or scarlet in the fall, and may drop off during the winter. In March and April you may see small, greenish-white flowers that become pea-sized white berries in the summer. The leaves are oval, lobed, approximately 2 inches long, and always come in threes.

Fire

Beginning in May, southern California enters its "fire season." The chaparral slows its growth and begins to dry out, the grass turns yellow, the humidity drops, and temperatures rise. Conditions intensify through June, July, and August. In the fall, they are compounded by hot, dry Santa Ana winds that blow in from the northeastern deserts. In the Angeles National Forest alone, more than one hundred fires are started by people each year. If you plan to ride during the "fire season," be aware of local fire danger and plan in advance your escape route if a fire erupts suddenly. Before you ride, check trail conditions and closures with the trail administering agency. Remember Smokey's motto: Only You Can Prevent Forest Fires.

If you see a fire:

- Return to your vehicle at once and leave the area.
- When in a safe place, dial 911 and report the location to local authorities.

Quicksand

Quicksand generally forms only under slow-moving or still water. To avoid riding into quicksand, stick to well-used trails and cross rivers and creeks where the water is moving quickly.

GUIDELINES FOR RIDING CONDUCT

- Greet everyone with a smile and friendly hello.

- Be of assistance when a need arises.

- Avoid loud talking or yelling.

- On streets and paved parking lots, pick up your animal's manure.

- On trails and in dirt parking lots, break up and scatter your animal's manure.

- Stay on trails. Cutting across switchbacks causes erosion.

- When meeting other trail users (including mountain bicyclists) on narrow trails, ask them to stand to the outside edge of the trail and continue talking, but do not make any sudden movements while you pass them. Since horses do not see well above them, it's helpful if other trail users can stand below the eye level of your horse.

- If your horses paw the ground, do not tie them to trees. Use a "tree-saver" or other padding to prevent your rope from cutting into the bark and damaging the tree.

LEGEND

Getting There

- **U** -- Easy access to parking area.

- **U U** -- Roads will accommodate most truck-trailer combinations.

- **U U U** -- Some narrow and/or winding roads. Will accommodate most truck-trailer combinations.

- **U U U U** -- Several miles of narrow and/or winding roads. Will be difficult for certain truck-trailer combinations. Follow recommendations in the trail text.

Parking

- **U** -- Lots of room to park and turn around; no backing up required.

- **U U** -- May require backing in or out; few obstacles, which are easy to see and avoid.

- **U U U** -- Some obstacles; space is adequate, but requires backing up.

- **U U U U** -- Small and/or limited parking that requires precise backing in or out. May be impossible for larger truck-trailer combinations.

Trail Difficulty

Trail difficulty has been divided into two components -- physical ability and training level -- to better define the trails listed. For example, a wide, smooth, but very steep trail would require a lot of physical ability, but not much training; a flat trail with many obstacles would require some training, but little physical stamina.

Physical Ability

- **U** -- Mostly flat, well-groomed, and well-marked trails. Good place to start the out-of-condition and/or inexperienced horse and rider.

- **U U** -- Obvious trails; may have small hillocks and gullies, and some rocks and/or sandy soil.

- **U U U** -- Horse and rider should be in good condition to enjoy this ride. Trails generally remote with varied footing and may not be well marked. Some moderate changes in elevation.

- **U U U U** -- Horse and rider must be in excellent condition to safely navigate and enjoy this ride. Trail blazing may be required. Elevation changes are abrupt and dramatic. Steep climbs and slippery and/or rocky trails should be expected.

Training Level

- **U** -- Safe for the relatively inexperienced horse and/or rider. Wide trail with few obstacles. No water crossings or bridges.

- **U U** -- Narrower trail with some obstacles such as fallen branches. Horse and rider should be accustomed to traffic. Horse should be able to back up if necessary to get out of a tight spot.

- **U U U** -- Horse and rider should be able to negotiate obstacles such as logs, small water crossings, or tree branches. Horse should respond accurately to rider's cues.

- **U U U U** -- Horse and rider must be well seasoned and able to adapt to the unexpected without losing control. Must be able to blaze new trails, cross water, and handle slippery and unstable footing.

Off-Road Vehicles & Mountain Bikes

- 🏁 -- Expect a few off-road vehicles (ORVs) and/or mountain bikes.

- 🏁 🏁 🏁 -- Trail frequented by off-road vehicles and/or mountain bikes. **Mountain bicyclists tend to ride in the mornings. In areas where cyclists frequent, plan your ride for later in the day to reduce the chance of encounters.**

Note: The Off-Road Vehicle/Mountain Bike listing appears only if applicable to the trail.

Maps

Interstates and Major Highways

Paved Road

Dirt Road

Trail

🅿 Parking

Note: Maps show several trails for each area. Your riding time will vary depending on the route and distance taken, but each area offers a minimum of 2 hours of riding.

ANZA-BORREGO DESERT STATE PARK
COYOTE CANYON

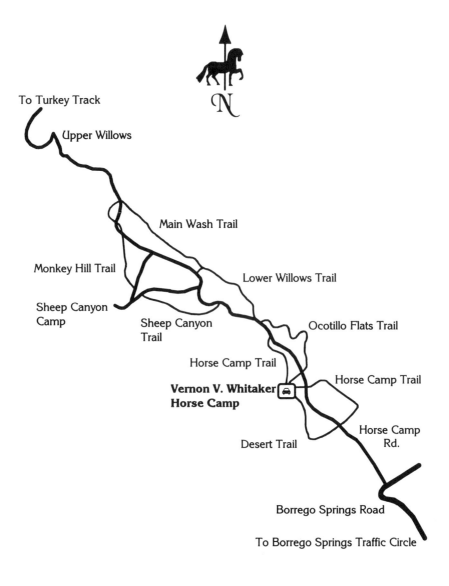

Anza-Borrego Desert State Park
Coyote Canyon
Vernon V. Whitaker Horse Camp

Located northeast of San Diego. For detailed maps and additional information, contact Anza-Borrego Desert State Park, P.O. Box 299, Borrego Springs CA 92004. Park Headquarters (619) 767-5311, Visitor Center program information (619) 767-4205, Wildflower Hotline (619) 767-4684. To make Horse Camp reservations, contact MISTIX State Park Reservation System at (800) 444-7275.

Hours
    Day Use .... 8 A.M. to Sunset
    Overnight... Check-out 12 noon
    COYOTE CANYON IS CLOSED June 15 through September 15
Fees
    Day Use .... $5 (pay camp host on arrival)
    Overnight.. $16/night (reservations recommended)
Getting There .... ♘ ♘
Parking... ♘ ♘
Hitching Rails/Corrals
    Day Use .... Yes/Yes. Arrange with camp host.
    Overnight.. Yes/Yes. Fee includes two corrals. Additional corrals are available for a fee.
Trail Difficulty
    Physical Ability .... ♘ ♘ to ♘ ♘ ♘ ♘
    Training Level .... ♘ ♘ to ♘ ♘ ♘ ♘
Elevation Gain
    Horse Camp to Lower Willows .... 230 feet in 2 miles
    Horse Camp to Upper Willows .... 875 feet in 11 miles
    Horse Camp to Sheep Canyon....................... 540 feet in 6.5 miles
Water .... People: Yes Horse: Yes
Toilets .... Yes, flush
Off-Road Vehicles.. Yes, 🏁 🏁 🏁

Directions:

To Borrego Springs Traffic Circle from the Los Angeles/San Bernardino area: Take Interstate 15 south to Temecula. Go east on State Highway 79 for 42 miles. Turn left onto County S2 and travel east for 5 miles. Turn left onto County S22 east (toward Ranchita) for 18 miles to Palm Canyon Drive. Make a right and continue 1.5 miles to the town of Borrego Springs.

To Borrego Springs Traffic Circle from the San Diego area: Take Interstate 15 north to County S4. Go east on County S4 for 5 miles, then turn left onto State Highway 67 north. Follow State Highway 67 for 10 miles to Ramona. Take State Highway 78 east for 15 miles to San Ysabel. Proceed north on State Highway 79 for 11 miles to County S2. Go east on County S2 for 5 miles and then turn left onto County S22 east (toward Ranchita). Travel 18 miles on County S22 to Palm Canyon Drive. Make a right and continue 1.5 miles to the town of Borrego Springs.

From Traffic Circle to Horse Camp: Make a right (north) on Borrego Springs Road and travel north 3.5 miles. Borrego Springs Road makes a sharp right and becomes Henderson Canyon Road. Just past this intersection, turn left (north) on the dirt Horse Camp Road and follow the signs approximately 4 miles to Horse Camp.

Description:

Here's a fantastic place to explore during March and April when the miracle of spring rain turns the dry land into a patchwork of yellow, red, pink, and purple bloom. On a recent visit, we rode for miles through a forest of flaming red ocotillo, cooled off in the perennial Coyote Creek, and ate dinner by crackling campfire under a brilliant canopy of stars. Not bad for what many people view as a barren, inhospitable land.

Other spring flowering plants found in the park include sand verbena -- bright pink lantana-like flowers; beaver tail cactus -- fluorescent purple-red blooms; barrel cactus -- brilliant yellow-green flowers; multicolored desert primrose; desert willow -- lavender or pink orchid-like blossoms; brittle-bush -- sunflower-shaped yellow flowers; smoke tree -- small, deep purple trumpet-shaped bloom; and the palo verde tree -- sweet pea-shaped yellow flowers. For more information about desert flora, stop at the Visitors Center, 1.5 miles west of the Borrego Springs Traffic Circle on Palm Canyon Drive. Hours: October through May 9 A.M. to 5 P.M. daily, June through September 9 A.M. to 5 P.M. Saturdays and Sundays only.

Although you can ride along any marked trail in the park, Coyote Canyon has been designated for horses and you'll find more trails to explore than time permits. Early morning and late afternoon offer the most dramatic flower viewing.

Photo by Laurie Berger

For the most part, trails are well marked, flat, sandy, and rocky. Unless your horse has exceptional hooves, shoes are a must. Watch out for the many-branched jumping chollo. From a distance, the copious spines glow a brilliant yellowish-white. Close up, branches are easily detached, hence the name jumping chollo. Carry a pair of pliers (needle nose are best), comb, or hemostat to remove any spines from your horse's legs. For stubborn spines, soak the skin with vinegar first.

Depending on the trail you choose, you'll ford Coyote Creek several times, offering your horse a chance to drink and both of you an opportunity to cool off. From mid-June through mid-September, desert bighorn sheep (*Borrego cimarron*) come down from the highlands to water, mate, and give birth in the Canyon. If you visit just before June 15 when the Canyon is closed to visitors, you may be lucky enough to spot some of these rare animals.

Spend a night or two if possible at Horse Camp. The facilities are Hilton-esque, including a solar shower, flush toilets, fire pits, picnic tables, forty corrals, horse washing area, and longeing area. With only ten campsites available, you'll need a reservation for weekend nights. Contact MISTIX, the State Park Reservation System, up to 56 days in advance.

When you ride in the desert, always carry plenty of water -- and drink it. Wear sunscreen, a hat, and sunglasses. Recorded temperatures have changed as much as 80 degrees during a 24-hour period, so bring appropriate clothing. Insect repellent for both horse and rider is a good idea, too. Give a wide berth to snakes and scorpions -- they will usually get out of your way if you let them. Mountain lions also make their home in the park. (See the precautions listed on page 13 of this guide.)

Deserts comprise nearly one-quarter of our state. A spring visit to Anza-Borrego Desert State Park is an excellent way to experience this unique and beautiful environment.

Big Rock Creek

To Pearblossom

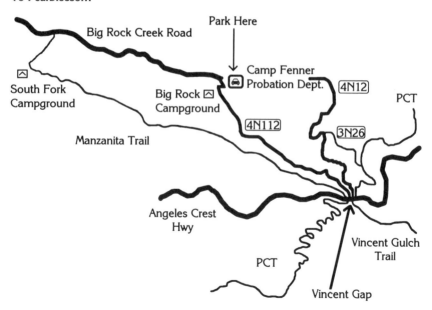

Big Rock Creek
Angeles National Forest Route 4N112

Located south of the Antelope Valley in the Angeles National Forest. For detailed maps and additional information, contact the Valyermo District Office, P.O. Box 15, 29835 Valyermo Road, Valyermo CA 93563, (805) 944-2187.

Hours	None
Fee	None
Getting There	♘ ♘
Parking	♘ ♘
Hitching Rails/Corrals	No/No
Trail Difficulty	
Physical Ability	♘ ♘ ♘
Training Level	♘ to ♘ ♘
Elevation Gain	1,600 feet in 2 miles to Vincent Gap. Start at 4,500 feet.
Water	People: No Horse: Seasonal
Toilets	Yes, pit (at Big Rock Creek Campground)

Directions:

From Los Angeles: Go north on the 14 Antelope Valley Freeway and exit at Pearblossom Highway. Go northeast 5 miles to Four Points. Turn right and continue on the 138 Pearblossom Highway 10 miles to Pearblossom. (From San Bernardino: Take Interstate 15 north to Cajon Junction. Exit at 138 Pearblossom Highway and go west 35 miles to Pearblossom.) Turn south on Longview Road. Go .6 miles and turn left (east) onto Ave. W, which veers south and becomes Valyermo Road. Go 7 miles to Big Rock Creek Road (National Forest Road 4N11) and turn right. Go 6 miles to the end of the road at Fenner Canyon Conservation Camp.

Description:

The sweet smell of sugar pine and constant twitter of birds will accompany you as you wind through an oak and pine forest. Angular slate-gray boulders grip the steep mountain slopes. Trees and rocks jut upward into a cobalt sky. When summer temperatures soar into the 100s and the city smog and noise are unbearable, this is the place to unwind. Bring a picnic lunch and plan to spend the day.

Park your rig across from the Camp Fenner baseball field and head up National Forest Route 4N112 toward Big Rock Creek Campground (about .25 miles up the road). During the summer, water is available here. Though steep, the trail is relatively smooth and wide enough to travel two or three abreast, making it a great place for a family ride. In the spring, you'll have several water crossings and the possibility of snow, so check trail conditions with the ranger station before starting out.

The trail ends at Vincent Gap on the Angeles Crest Highway. From here you have several trail options including the Manzanita Trail to South Fork Campground, the Pacific Crest Trail, the Vincent Gulch Trail, and National Forest Routes 4N12 and 3N26.

Big Rock Creek Camp, a private camp near South Fork Campground, offers overnight equestrian camping. Tent camping is $9 per person per night, and RV sites are $20 per night for two people (additional charge for extra people). There is no fee for horses tied to the trailer overnight. If the camp has a stall available, the fee is $3 per night. Contact the camp for further information and reservations: Big Rock Creek Camp, P.O. Box 66, Valyermo CA 93563, (805) 944-9005, fax (805) 944-9011.

Big Rock Creek makes a great summer destination for the entire family.

Big Sycamore Canyon
Northern Portion

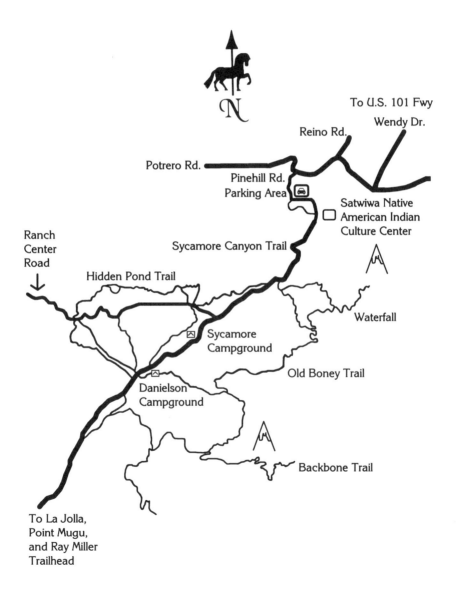

To U.S. 101 Fwy

Wendy Dr.

Reino Rd.

Potrero Rd.

Pinehill Rd.
Parking Area

Satwiwa Native
American Indian
Culture Center

Sycamore Canyon Trail

Ranch
Center
Road

Hidden Pond Trail

Waterfall

Sycamore
Campground

Old Boney Trail

Danielson
Campground

Backbone Trail

To La Jolla,
Point Mugu,
and Ray Miller
Trailhead

Big Sycamore Canyon
Northern Portion

Located in the Santa Monica Mountain National Recreation Area (SMMNRA), a unit of the National Park Service, managed by the California Department of Parks and Recreation (CDPR). For detailed maps and additional information, contact CDPR, 1925 Las Virgenes Rd., Calabasas CA 91302, (818) 880-0350. Information about Rancho Sierra Vista/Satwiwa can be obtained from the SMMNRA Unit of the National Park Service, 30401 Agoura Road, Suite 100, Agoura Hills CA 91301, (818) 597-9192 x201.

Hours .... 8 A.M. to Sunset
Fee .... None
Getting There .... U
Parking .... U
Hitching Rails/Corrals
    Parking area .... No/No
    Sycamore Campground .... Yes/Yes
    Danielson Campground .... Yes/No
Trail Difficulty
    Physical Ability .... U U
    Training Level .... U U to U U U
Elevation Loss .... -900 feet in 8 miles
Water .... People: Yes Horse: Yes
Toilets .... Yes, pit
Bicyclists .... Yes, 🚩 🚩 🚩

Directions:

Take the U.S. 101 Ventura Freeway to Newbury Park; exit at Wendy Drive and turn south. Travel 2.9 miles to Potrero Road; turn right (west). Travel .6 miles to the stop sign (intersection with Reino Road); take left (south) fork. Continue .5 miles to Pinehill Road; turn left (south). You are entering Rancho Sierra Vista/Satwiwa. Travel .5 miles to the parking area.

Description:

You'll have plenty of loop trails to choose from in Big Sycamore Canyon.   Take a picnic lunch and plan to stop at either Sycamore or Danielson Campgrounds, or for the ambitious, at the Ray Miller trailhead at the Pacific Ocean.

From   the parking area, head out the exit, cross Pinehill Road, and take the left fork of Pinehill Trail.   This short path takes you along a grassy knoll with a panoramic view of the parking area and former Moorpark College Demonstration Ranch.   The trail ends where Pinehill Road passes the Satwiwa Native American Indian Cultural Center.   Turn right and follow the road for .3 miles to the boundary between Rancho Sierra Vista/Satwiwa and Point Mugu State Park.   The road now becomes Big Sycamore Canyon Trail and is paved.   At this point, you can take a well-marked trail to your left and explore the upper eastern portion of the canyon or head toward the ocean.

The first mile into Big Sycamore Canyon is along a steep, paved road. You'll lose 350 feet -- close to a 6% grade -- in this mile, but after that the trails are gently rolling. Part way down the grade you can fill your canteen at fire hydrant #3 if you didn't already do so at the parking area. At the bottom of the grade you'll find the Hidden Pond Trail on your right, a few yards past fire hydrant #5. There's a pit toilet here if needed.

Hidden Pond Trail roughly parallels Big Sycamore Canyon Road taking you along gently rolling grassland and new growth chaparral. Follow the trail for 1 mile until it intersects with Ranch Center Road (dirt). Here, you have several options: (1) Take Ranch Center Road to the right and circle around to Big Sycamore Canyon Road, (2) Take Ranch Center Road to the left and connect to Big Sycamore Canyon Road, (3) Take the right trail and continue on the Hidden Pond Trail looping back to Ranch Center Road or Big Sycamore Canyon Road, or (4) Cross Ranch Center Road and ride 1 mile to Danielson Campground.

Danielson and Sycamore Campgrounds are located in the heart of the canyon. Sycamore, as the name suggests, is nestled in a grove of huge sycamore trees. The trees, which provide cool summer shade, produce beautiful color in the fall. Sycamore has pipe corrals, hitching rails, tables, pit toilets, fire pits, stoves, and running water. E.T.I. Corral 63 donated many of the equestrian facilities, which are available for group camping. If you'd like to camp, contact the California Department of Parks and Recreation for information about fees and reservations.

From Danielson, you have access to the Old Boney Trail and the Backbone Trail, which traverses most of the Santa Monica Mountains from east to west. Or you can continue down the canyon, heading west toward the La Jolla area, Point Mugu, and the Ray Miller trailhead.

After your ride, plan a visit to the Rancho Sierra Vista/ Satwiwa Site and Cultural Center. A portion of the site has been designated as the Satwiwa Native American Indian Natural Area, which means Native Indian descendants may gather here to perpetuate traditions. Horses are not allowed in the natural area, so leave them at your trailer and walk over for a visit.

"Horsemanship is the skill

of working with the horse.

Equitation is the art."

Jennifer Ormerod
Crown Valley Horsemanship Center
Acton, CA

Browns Creek Park/Browns Canyon

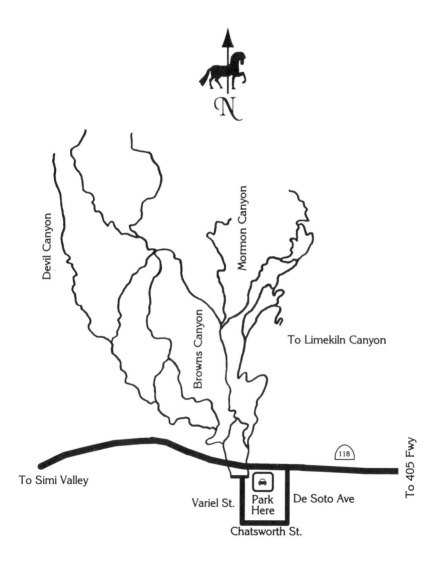

Browns Creek Park/Browns Canyon

Located in the northwestern corner of the San Fernando Valley in the foothills of the Santa Susana Mountains. For detailed maps and additional information, contact Los Angeles City Parks and Recreation, Valley Region Headquarters, 6335 Woodley Ave., Van Nuys CA 91406, (818) 756-8060.

Hours	None
Fees	None
Getting There	U
Parking	U U
Hitching Rails/Corrals	No/No
Trail Difficulty	
Physical Ability	U U U to U U U U
Training Level	U U to U U U
Elevation Gain	Depends on route and distance. Start at 500 feet.
Water	People: No Horse: Seasonal
Toilets	No

Directions:

Take the 118 Ronald Reagan Freeway (formerly the Simi Valley Freeway) to the San Fernando Valley; exit at De Soto Avenue and turn south. Travel .6 miles to Chatsworth Street and turn right (west). Travel .3 miles to Variel Street; turn right (north) and continue two blocks to Rinaldi. Park in the dirt lot on the northeast corner of Rinaldi and Variel.

Description:

Popular with local equestrians, Browns Creek Park and Browns Canyon provide many miles of trails with excellent views of the San Fernando Valley and 3,747-foot Oat Mountain to the north. One resident said he'd ridden the area for 2 years and still found new trails to explore.

From the parking area, ride due north over the hill and then veer right, down into Browns Creek Park. From here you have several trail choices leading generally north toward Oat Mountain. If the main trail access into Browns Creek Park is closed for freeway construction, go back to the parking lot and take the groomed bridle path west on Rinaldi; then turn right (north) on Canoga. Cross under the freeway to the top of the hill. Veer right on the fire road to access Browns Creek Park or take one of the other trails available from this point. The extensive web of interconnected trails includes dirt roads, fire roads, and trails.

If you visit in the spring you'll find a riot of flowers including bright red paintbrush, ground-pink (a star-shaped flower with fringed petals, which hides in the shade of other shrubs), and creamy white elderberry blossoms. Cottonwood tree seed pods, which look like green grapes, open in the spring, sending out a profusion of fluffy cotton-like fibers, similar to the cattail. In the heat of summer and early fall, plan a picnic under the eucalyptus, sycamore, alder, and cottonwood trees that line Browns Creek. In October, the sycamore leaves turn several shades of red and gold.

For a spectacular ride for the fit and experienced horse and rider, try Devils Canyon. Since much of the trail is in the creek bed, your horse must be water-wise and able to negotiate rocks and small boulders. If you choose this route, ask a local rider about trail conditions before starting out.   Winter and spring rains often make this route dangerous or impassable.

Browns Creek Park and Canyon are beautiful places to experience the changing seasons. With their splendid views and expansive trail systems, you'll return again and again.

Cheeseboro Canyon
Palo Comado Canyon

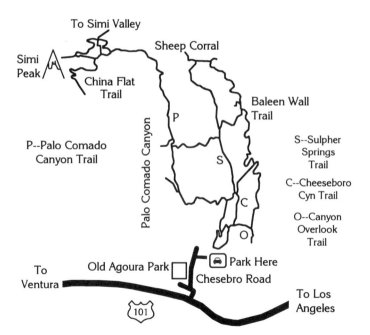

Cheeseboro Canyon
Palo Comado Canyon

Located in the Santa Monica Mountain National Recreation Area (SMMNRA), a unit of the National Park Service. For detailed maps and additional information, contact SMMNRA Unit of the National Park Service, 30401 Agoura Road, Suite 100, Agoura Hills CA 91301, (818) 597-9192 x201, or the Santa Monica Mountains Conservancy Parklands Information (310) 456-7040.

Hours	8 A.M. to Sunset (parking lot hours). Trails may be accessed at any time if you park at entrance sign.
Fee	None
Getting There	U
Parking	U U
Hitching Rails/Corrals	No/No
Trail Difficulty	
Physical Ability	U U to U U U U
Training Level	U U to U U U U
Elevation Gain	Depends on route and distance. Start at 1,000 feet.
Parking area to Simi Peak	1,400 feet in 8 miles
Parking area to Sheep Corral	650 feet in 6 miles
Water	People: No Horse: Seasonal
Toilets	No
Bicyclists	Yes,

Directions:

Take the U.S. 101 Ventura Freeway to Agoura Hills and exit at Chesebro Road. Go north .2 miles to a stop sign. Turn right at the stop sign and continue on Chesebro Road .7 miles to the Cheeseboro Canyon entrance sign. Turn right and travel .4

miles to the parking lot. If the lot is full, circle around, go back to the entrance sign, and park there.

Description:

Within the 2,147 acres of Cheeseboro Canyon and the 2,329 acres of Palo Comado Canyon, you'll find several days of superb riding. The Chumash Indians lived here for thousands of years and evidence of their existence still remains.

The two canyon sites contain several plant communities including riparian woodland, the habitat along a stream or pond. The continuous source of water, either on the surface or just below ground, is needed by the plants that live here: maple, alder, stream orchid, scarlet monkey flower, cottonwood, coast live oak, California blackberry, and poison oak, to name a few. Southern oak woodland, also found here, is dominated by coast live oak trees. Chaparral is the largest plant community in the sites, with plants adapted to dry rocky soil, hot summers, and limited rainfall. Most chaparral shrubs have the ability to crown-sprout after the top is killed by fire or physical removal.

You'll have three main trails to choose from: Palo Comado Canyon Trail, Cheeseboro Canyon Trail, and Baleen Wall Trail that follows the mountain ridge east of Cheeseboro Canyon. Several cross trails connect these three, providing plenty of loop riding opportunities. You'll find riding for all levels of ability at the sites, from the gentle main trail up Cheeseboro Canyon to the climb along the Baleen Wall.

If you choose the Cheeseboro Canyon Trail, you'll ride through rolling grasslands and chaparral before heading into the shade of the riparian woodland community. You can loop over to the Canyon Overlook Trail or the Sulphur Springs Trail on your way up the canyon. Approximately 2 miles up Cheeseboro Canyon Trail, you'll find two or three picnic tables where you can enjoy a saddlebag lunch and relax under a cooling oak tree canopy. Be sure to tie your horse safely where he will not damage protected plant life or tree roots. After lunch, you can continue north up Cheeseboro Canyon Trail to Sheep Corral or take the cutoff to Baleen Wall Trail and circle back to the parking lot. Or take one of several cutoffs into Palo Comado Canyon that goes to China Flats, Albertson Motorway, and into Simi Valley. The Baleen Wall Trail is steep in parts and not recommended for green horses and riders.

All trails are well marked, and some are wide enough to ride three abreast.   The area is a favorite of mountain bicyclists. Cheeseboro and Palo Comado Canyons are great places for a family ride and picnic.   During the summer, plan a breakfast or supper ride to avoid the midday heat.

News Flash -- Completed June 1995: the Old Agoura Park, located on the northwest corner of Chesebro Canyon Road and Driver Avenue.   Administered jointly by the city of Agoura Hills and the SMMNRA, this equestrian park offers a riding arena, turn-out corral, hitching rail, and automatic waterer. If you like, you can park here and take a flat .7-mile trail to the entrance to Cheeseboro Canyon.

Do you know a great trail?

Would you like to contribute
to the next volume?

Please fill out and mail in the form on page 127.

With your help, the next volume will be even
bigger and better.

Chino Hills State Park
Eastern Section

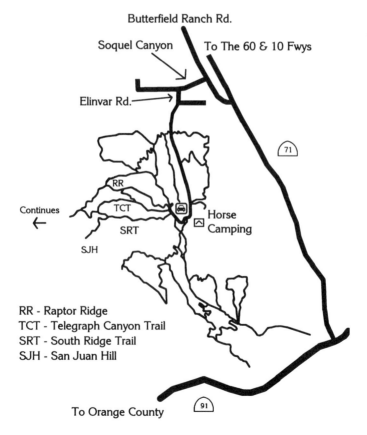

Butterfield Ranch Rd.

Soquel Canyon

To The 60 & 10 Fwys

Elinvar Rd.

71

RR

TCT

Continues

SRT

Horse
Camping

SJH

RR - Raptor Ridge
TCT - Telegraph Canyon Trail
SRT - South Ridge Trail
SJH - San Juan Hill

To Orange County   91

Chino Hills State Park

A 13,000-acre state park in Riverside County near Corona and Norco. For detailed maps and additional information, contact Chino Hills District Office, 1879 Jackson St., Riverside CA 92504, (909) 780-6222, 8 A.M. to 4:30 P.M. Monday through Friday.

Hours
 Day Use .... 8 A.M. to Sunset
 Overnight.. Check-out 12 noon
Fees
 Day Use .... $5 per vehicle (Pay at entrance station. Exact change is appreciated.)
Overnight .... $12/night (first-come, first-served)
Getting There .... ♘ ♘
Parking.. ♘
Hitching Rails/Corrals
 Day Use .... Yes/No
 Overnight.. Yes/Yes
Trail Difficulty
 Physical Ability .... ♘ ♘ to ♘ ♘ ♘ ♘
 Training Level .... ♘ to ♘ ♘ ♘
Elevation Gain .... Depends on route and distance. San Juan Hill is 1,781 feet.
Water .... People: Yes Horse: Yes
Toilets .... Yes, pit
Bicyclists .... Yes, ⚐

Directions:

The park entrance is west of the 71 Corona Expressway, approximately 12 miles south of the 60 Pomona Freeway and

3.5 miles north of the 91 Riverside Freeway. From the 71 Corona Expressway, turn west on Butterfield Ranch Road. Travel 3.2 miles to Soquel Road and turn left. Continue .6 miles to Elinvar; turn left. Elinvar doglegs and becomes Sapphire. Just past the dogleg is the dirt road park entrance.

Note: At press time, freeway construction had caused some detours of the 71 Corona Expressway. If you are concerned about locating the Butterfield Ranch Road turnoff, call (800) 718-7328 for construction information. When freeway construction is completed, you'll need to contact the Chino Hills District Office for updated directions to the park, including which freeway offramp to take.

Description:

Sixty-five miles of trails and stellar horse and picnicking facilities will keep you coming back to Chino Hills State Park again and again.

Rolling grass-covered hills dotted with walnut, oak, and sycamore trees await you in this island of undeveloped land located less than 10 miles from Norco and Corona. The Gabrielino Indians once lived here, hunting and traveling along seasonal creeks. The Hills for Everyone Trail, a hiking-only path, follows one of these old Indian paths. Wildlife is abundant in the park, including coyotes, bobcats, deer, rattlesnakes, badgers, pond turtles, owls, and golden eagles. On a recent trip, we saw several red-tailed hawks riding the thermals.

The day-use staging area is located on a grassy knoll overlooking the western section of the park. Here you'll find pristine chemical toilets and water troughs clean enough to bathe in. Park Aid Dennis, a former endurance rider, takes special pride in maintaining the equestrian facilities. Several picnic tables are available, shaded from the hot summer sun by a lattice canopy. Tie your horse to one of the very sturdy hitching rails while you enjoy a tailgate lunch or dinner.

Four categories of trails exist: wide dirt roads; trails 60 or more inches wide designated for riding, hiking, and bicycling; trails 60 or more inches wide designated for riding and hiking only; and hiking-only trails that are less than 60 inches wide. With abundant wide trails and rolling terrain, this is an excellent place to condition a young or soft horse and rider.

There are three first-come, first-served horse camping sites in the park. Try to arrive midweek or by early Friday afternoon to ensure a spot (avoid holiday weekends if possible). Each site includes a 12-by-24-foot pipe corral, fire pit, picnic table, and drinking water. Chemical toilets are nearby. The park allows up to eight people and two horses per site. Additional horses may be tied to your trailer or in your own portable stalls. Bring equipment to clean up after your horse.

Summers are hot in the park. The best time to visit is during fall, winter, or spring when the wildflowers bloom.

Forks of the Kern River

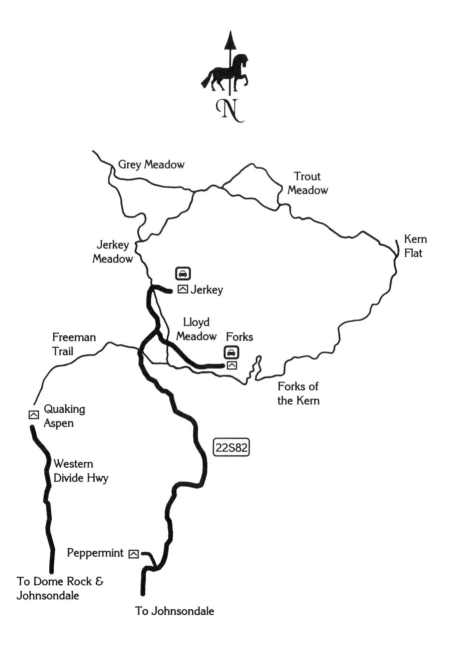

Forks of the Kern River
Jerkey Campground
Forks Campground

Contributed by Jennifer and Rick Fuller

Located 35 miles north of Lake Isabella in the Sequoia National Forest. For detailed maps and additional information, contact Tule River Ranger District Office, 32588 Hwy. 190, Springville CA 93265, (209) 539-2607.

Hours .... None
Fees .... Contact the district
         office, or the National
         Recreation Reservation
         System at (800) 280-2267.
Getting There .... **U U U** **
Parking .... **U U**
Hitching Rails/Corrals
     Day Use .... No/Yes
     Overnight .... No/Yes
Trail Difficulty
     Physical Ability .... **U U** to **U U U U**
     Training Level .... **U U** to **U U U U**
Elevation
     Forks Campground .... Elevation 5,750 feet
     Jerkey Campground .... Elevation 6,500 feet
     Forks Campground to Forks of the Kern
         River -- Loss .... -1,150 feet in 2 miles
     Forks of the Kern River to
         Kern Flat -- Gain .... 480 feet in 6 miles
     Freeman Creek Trail from Forks Campground
         to Quaking Aspen -- Gain .... 1,500 feet in 5.5 miles
     Jerkey to Lloyd Meadows -- Gain .... 750 feet in 3 miles
Water
     Jerkey Campground .... People: Yes Horse: Yes
     Forks Campground .... *People: No* Horse: No
Toilets .... Yes, pit (bring toilet paper)

Directions:

Take the 14 Antelope Valley Freeway north of Mojave to State Highway 178 (to Lake Isabella); go west. Continue 32 miles to Sierra Way; turn right (north) toward Kernville and Johnsondale. Travel 37 miles. One mile past Johnsondale turn right at the sign, "Camp Whitsett -- Lower Peppermint -- Lloyd Meadows Trailheads." You are now on National Forest Road 22S82. Continue 19.2 miles. Turn right to Forks Campground (2.5 miles), or continue 2 miles on 22S82 to Jerkey Campground. **The road between Kernville and Johnsondale is somewhat narrow and winding.

Description:

Balmy days, crisp nights, and the solitude of riding in the heart of the wilderness await you. Pitch your tent under a towering sequoia (*Sequoia dendron giganteum*). Roast fresh-caught rainbow trout for dinner under a star-studded sky. Fall asleep to the call of an owl rippling through the quiet. If the John Muir experience excites you, then Forks and Jerkey trailhead campgrounds are A-list destinations.

Photo by Jennifer Fuller

Forks Campground has four large, sturdy corrals; Jerkey has five. Both campgrounds offer pit toilets, picnic tables, and an occasional herd of cows that wanders through camp -- and stays for dinner! Camps are designed for stays of 1 or 2 nights only. For longer stays, try Peppermint or Quaking Aspen Campgrounds. Wilderness and campfire permits are required. Contact the Tule River Ranger District Office.

American black bears (*Ursus americans*) inhabit the Sequoia National Forest and bear/human encounters are on the rise. Here are a few pointers to help prevent a disaster:

- Don't leave food out -- including sweet feed for your horses.
- Keep all food tightly wrapped.
- Store food containers out of sight. Bears know what ice chests look like and what's inside. Hide them in your trailer tack room or inside your truck covered with a blanket.
- If you encounter a bear on the trail, stay calm and give it plenty of room.

With the variety of trails available, riding can be as vigorous or gentle as you like. For the adventurous, pack your fishing pole and take Forks of the Kern Trail, a scenic 2-mile ride down the canyon to the Kern River. The trail is good, but narrow and rocky in places. If you continue to Kern Flat, check river crossing conditions with the ranger station before starting out.

History buffs should try the Freeman Creek Trail -- an easy ride along grassy meadows -- to see the George Bush Sequoia tree. The 2,000-year-old tree was dedicated in 1992 to commemorate Bush's visit to the Freeman Grove and his proclamation to protect giant sequoia groves in California.

Forks of the Kern River is a wonderful midsummer retreat from the heat and bustle of the city.

Liebre Gulch Road

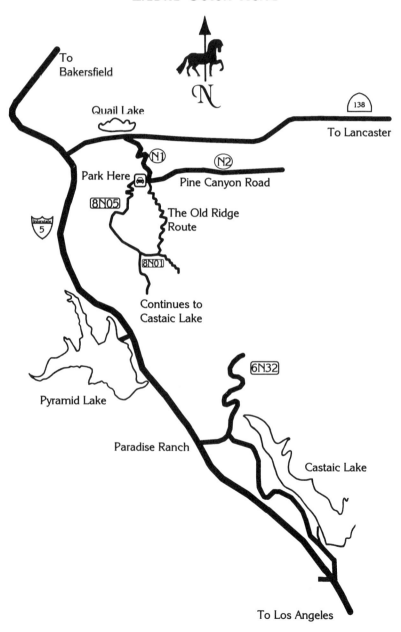

LiEbRE GulcH RoAd
ANqElEs NATioNAl ForEST RouTE 8N05

Located east of Gorman (40 miles north of the San Fernando Valley) in the Angeles National Forest. For detailed maps and additional information, contact Saugus District Office, 30800 Bouquet Canyon Road, Saugus CA 91350, (805) 252-9710.

Hours	None
Fee	None
Getting There	♘ ♘
Parking	♘ ♘
Hitching Rails/Corrals	No/No
Trail Difficulty	
Physical Ability	♘ ♘ ♘ ♘
Training Level	♘ ♘ to ♘ ♘ ♘
Elevation Loss	
From parking area to bottom of gulch	-750 feet in .5 miles
From parking area to Jct. with 8N01	-1,000 feet in 3 miles
Water	People: No Horse: No
Toilets	No
Off-Road Vehicles	Yes, 🏁

Directions:

Take Interstate 5 to the Gorman/Hungry Valley area; exit at State Highway 138/Palmdale-Lancaster. Go east on State Highway 138 for 4.3 miles to Ridge Route (County Road N2). Turn right (south) onto Ridge Route/County Road N2. Travel 2 miles up a curvy road to the intersection of Ridge Route/County Road N2, the Old Ridge Route, and Pine Canyon Road. You'll see a large wooden sign giving the history of the Old Ridge Route road. Park in the field to your right.

Description:

Start your ride at the top of a grassy knoll and ride down a fairly steep canyon for approximately .5 miles before the trail levels off. Pine trees and several varieties of oaks provide shade. The maple syrup-like aroma of buckwheat mixed with the pungent odor of decaying oak leaves wafts on the breeze. Manzanita, acacia, and many native shrubs grow along the hillsides. You'll see a variety of birds, including a flock of noisy blue jays.

The trail is wide and fairly smooth, but you'll cross several streambeds, which carry water in the spring. Although it does not appear to be much used by off-road vehicles, 8N05 is designated for them, so be prepared to share. The scenery is worth the occasional 4WD or all-terrain vehicle, and you'll be able to hear their approach in plenty of time to get off the road.

Two riding options exist depending on your time and physical condition. For the easier ride, continue down the canyon as long as you wish, then return the same way. Be sure you and your horse have enough energy for the .5-mile climb back out. More conditioned riders and horses can ride down the canyon approximately 2.5 miles, making a left at Road 8N01 (it's well marked). Approximately 1 mile long, 8N01 climbs out of Liebre Gulch and connects to the Old Ridge Route. Make a left here and head back to your trailer, approximately 5 miles. The Old Ridge Route is flat with paving remnants dating back to 1915, the year it was built. Considered an engineering feat in its day, it cut 44 miles off the previous route through these mountains. You may pass an occasional car taking the historical drive, but for the most part, you'll have the road to yourself. This ride should take you approximately three and one-half hours.

For people who enjoy riding in remote areas, Liebre Gulch is the perfect spot. Although steep at the beginning, the trail is wide enough to ride two abreast and offers great scenery and beautiful blue skies.

Little Tujunga Canyon

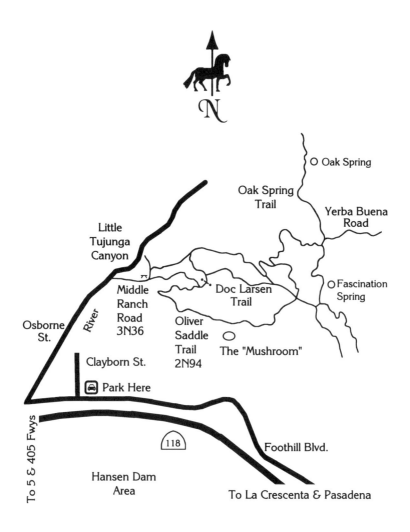

Little Tujunga Canyon
Hansen Dam Area
Oliver Saddle Trail
Oak Spring Trail
Doc Larsen Trail

Located northeast of the San Fernando Valley in the Angeles National Forest. For detailed maps and additional information, contact Tujunga District Office, 12371 N. Little Tujunga Canyon Road, San Fernando CA 91342, (818) 899-1900.

Hours	None
Fee	None
Getting There	♆
Parking	♆ ♆
Hitching Rails/Corrals	No/No
Trail Difficulty	
Physical Ability	♆ ♆ ♆ to ♆ ♆ ♆ ♆
Training Level	♆ ♆ ♆
Elevation Gain	Depends on route and distance. Start at 1,000 feet.
Parking area to the "Mushroom"	1,023 feet in 3 miles
Parking area to Fascination Spring	1,000 feet in 4 miles
Water	People: No Horse: Seasonal
Toilets	No

Directions:

Take the 210 Pasadena Freeway to Lake View Terrace. If traveling eastbound, exit at Osborne, and turn left at the bottom of the offramp onto Foothill Blvd. Travel approximately .5 miles to Clayborn; turn left and park in the large dirt area on the northeast corner. If traveling westbound, exit at Wheatland and turn right; turn left on Foothill Blvd. Travel approximately 1 mile to Clayborn; turn right and park in the large dirt area on the northeast corner.

Description:

This is a popular access point to several miles of trails in the Angeles National Forest including the Doc Larsen, Oak Spring, and Oliver Saddle Trails. The Doc Larsen Trail is named in honor of the retired veterinarian who built and maintains it.

Spring brings a variety of wildflowers to this area, including caterpillar phacelia (which looks like purple flowered fiddleneck), scotch broom, wild cucumber, chia, mustard, and sage. As the season progresses, acacias send out their cottony seeds, elderberry trees set their tiny fruit, and the tips of the chamise turn creamy white with bloom. When the Santa Ana winds arrive in the fall and blow the smog out of the San Fernando Valley, the views are incredible. Winter and spring rains can turn the Little Tujunga Creek into an impassable thundering torrent, so verify trail conditions with the ranger station before starting out.

To reach the trails from the Clayborn parking area, the general route is across Little Tujunga Creek, then alongside it for approximately 1 mile until you reach Middle Ranch Road/National Forest Road 3N36. The exact route along Little Tujunga Creek changes seasonally, but is easy to find. The creekside trail is mostly rock and gravel and can be a challenge to the in-experienced horse. Creek crossings are rocky and may be knee deep or more. As the season progresses and the water level drops, this section becomes easier to traverse.

At Middle Ranch Road/National Forest Road 3N36, turn right (east) and ride a short distance to where the road doglegs to the left. Here, nestled under a canopy of oaks is the perfect place for a picnic -- and someone has kindly provided a table.

On your right is a marked trail leading into a forest of oaks. The trail winds along a tributary stream for approximately 1 mile before intersecting with the Oliver Saddle Trail (National Forest Road 2N94). If you turn right, you'll climb approximately 1 mile through chaparral-covered hills to the ridge where the landmark domed-shaped, concrete "mushroom" is located.

If you turn left at the Oliver Saddle Trail intersection and follow the wide "fire road" for approximately .5 miles, you'll come to the Middle Ranch locked gate. Ride around the gate and continue to the top of a rise to a "T" intersection, turn right. You are now on the Doc Larsen Trail. You'll come to a water trough, some tie rails, and a yellow pipe with "Doc Larsen" written on it. Both the Doc Larsen and Oliver Saddle Trails connect to the Oak Spring Trail.

By turning left at the "T" intersection, you'll loop back to the picnic table, an easy 2-hour ride from beginning to end.

Little Tujunga Canyon offers great close-to-home riding for residents of the San Fernando Valley and good trails and easy freeway access for out-of-area visitors.

Mojave Narrows Regional Park

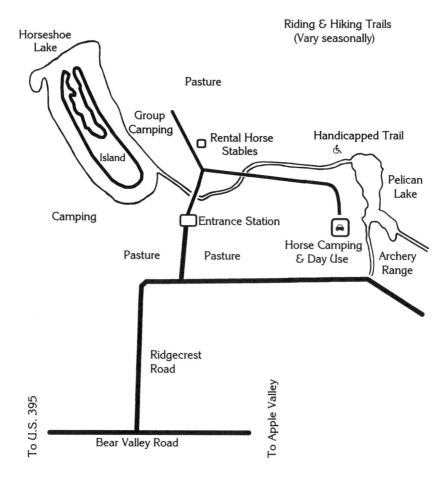

Mojave Narrows Regional Park

An 840-acre park located in Victorville (120 miles east of Los Angeles, 35 miles north of San Bernardino). Address: 18000 Yates Road, P.O. Box 361, Victorville CA 92392, (619) 245-2226. Equestrian Center Information (619) 244-1644.

Hours .... 7:30 A.M. to Sunset. Closed
                                                                    Tuesdays.
Fee
    Day Use
        Weekdays................................ $4 per vehicle
        Weekends .... $5 per vehicle
    Overnight Use .... $10 per night, no
                                                                    hookups
    Dogs... $1 per dog, must be
                                                                    leashed at all times
Getting There .... U
Parking... U
Hitching Rails/Corrals .... Contact the Equestrian
                                                                    Center for information
                                                                    regarding use of facilities.
Trail Difficulty
    Physical Ability .... U U
    Training Level .... U U
Elevation Gain .... None. Start at 2,700 feet.
Water .... People: Yes Horse: Yes
Toilets .... Yes, flush

Directions:

    From San Fernando/Santa Clarita Valleys: Go north on the 14 Antelope Valley Freeway; exit at Pearblossom Highway. Go northeast 5 miles to Four Points. Turn right and continue on the 138 Pearblossom Highway for 19.5 miles. Turn left onto State

Highway 18 and travel 20.2 miles. Turn right onto U.S. 395 for 1.6 miles. Turn left at Bear Valley Road and go 7.5 miles. Turn left at Ridgecrest Road and go 2.7 miles. Turn left into the park.

From Los Angeles and San Bernardino: Take Interstate 15 north through the Cajon Pass and exit at Bear Valley Road (17.3 miles north of Cajon Junction). Go east 4.5 miles. Turn left (north) at Ridgecrest Road and go 2.7 miles. Turn left into the park.

Description:

Nestled in a wide section of the Mojave riverbed and surrounded by water-eroded cliffs, Mojave Narrows Regional Park is a high-desert oasis for riding, camping, and fishing. Horses and cattle graze on irrigated pastures lining the road to the entrance station. Beyond the pastures, a forest of cottonwood and willow trees awaits you and your mount. Follow the signs to the "equestrian area" and park your trailer next to the tree-lined stream that feeds into Pelican Lake; you'll have a shady place to picnic after your ride. Tables and fire pits are provided, or set up folding chairs next to the stream.

Due east and south of the equestrian campground/day-use area is an archery range, which you'll want to avoid. A little north of the Pelican Lake dam is the nature trail for the handicapped, which equestrians can also use. The Rotary Club is rebuilding the bridge, so this way may not be passable. A bit further on, you'll find several trails leading off to your right. Pick one and explore.

Enter the cool forest and ride along a network of trails that change with the seasons and flow of the river. The only noises you'll hear are the soft plop of your horse's hooves and the occasional rumble of a train west of the park. A cool breeze rustles through cattails, water reeds, and thick bunches of marsh grass.   Burnt orange and bright blue dragonflies catch the sunlight as they zip around looking for food.

The park is a wildlife refuge, home to several varieties of water fowl and other animals. Mallard and canvas back ducks are common, as are turkey vultures. In the fall, Canada and snow geese arrive to spend the winter. Trails are flat, but laced with fallen logs and tree roots to step over. Depending on where you ride and the time of year, you'll have water to cross. To avoid quicksand, stick to well-used crossings and cross where the water is moving quickly. Quicksand generally forms only under slow-moving or still water.

When summer temperatures soar to 100 degrees and above, you'll always find a cool spot to ride and picnic at Mojave Narrows Regional Park.

Montaña de Oro State Park

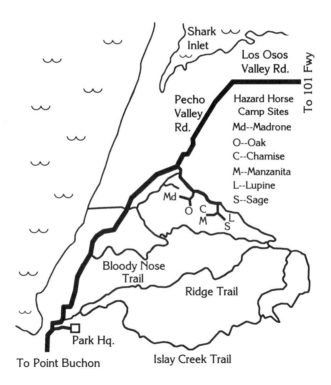

Montaña de Oro State Park
Hazard Canyon Horse Camps

An 8,000-acre park on the southern edge of Morro Bay. For detailed maps and additional information, contact Montaña de Oro State Park, Pecho Valley Road, Los Osos CA 93402, (805) 528-0513. To make reservations, contact MISTIX State Park Reservation System at (800) 444-7275.

Hours
    Day Use .... 8 A.M. to Sunset
    Overnight.. Check-out 12 noon

Fees
    Day Use .... None
    Overnight.. $16/night for family camp sites Lupine, Sage, Chamise, and Manzanita. Includes two horses per site. Additional horses (tied to trailer) $2 per night. $60/night for group camps Oak and Madrone. 7-25 horses per site.

Getting There .... ♘ ♘ ♘

Parking.. ♘ ♘

Hitching Rails/Corrals
    Day Use .... No/No
    Overnight.. No/Yes. Each family campsite includes two one-horse stalls. Additional corrals are not available. (See text for detailed information.)

Trail Difficulty
    Physical Ability .... ♘ ♘ to ♘ ♘ ♘ ♘
    Training Level .... ♘ ♘ to ♘ ♘ ♘ ♘

Elevation Gain .... Depends on route and distance. Start at sea level.

Water .... *People: No* Horse: Yes

Toilets .... Yes, pit

Directions:

From Los Angeles, head north on U.S. 101 through Santa Barbara and Santa Maria.   Approximately 16 miles north of Arroyo Grande, exit U.S. 101 at Los Osos Valley Road.   Turn west.   After 11 miles, Los Osos Valley Road becomes Pecho Valley Road. Continue another 1.2 miles into the park. Turn left at the "Horse Camps" sign and follow the signs to your camp.

Description:

Have you ever dreamed of galloping down an empty beach, hair whipped back by the salt mist; your horse splashing through foam-edged water, each hoof sending up an arc of glittering spray?   Did the scenes of Alex Ramsey (played by Kelly Reno) and The Black (played by Arabian horse Cass Olé) dancing through the surf on that deserted island in *The Black Stallion* make your blood rush?   Then, Montaña de Oro State Park is the place for you.   With 7 miles of shoreline, you can turn your fantasies into reality.

The horse camps are located approximately .5 miles from the shore and the trail is clearly marked. On the way, you'll ride through a grove of eucalyptus trees planted by Alexander Hazard in the late 1930s. Hazard, for whom the canyon was named, hoped to turn the canyon into a prosperous lumber farm. Unfortunately, eucalyptus wood proved unsatisfactory for commercial use, but the trees remain -- a shady respite from hot spring and fall sun. Other park trails climb through thick chaparral, wind along ridge tops, then drop down into other canyons. Canyon trails are fairly well marked, although narrow in places. Ticks, including those that carry Lyme disease, abound in the chaparral. Dress accordingly and use a tick repellent on both your horse and yourself. When you ride in the ocean, be aware that receding water undermines the sand beneath your horse's feet. This can be unsettling for your horse.

The one-lane dirt road down to the horse camps is steep in parts, but only about .5 miles long. Poison oak and poison hemlock surround the camps, but flies, mosquitoes, and bees are noticeably absent. In the early summer you'll see lots of "mom" and "pop" quail followed by a dozen or more chicks. Raccoons frequent the camps at night. Be sure to lock away all food and put all garbage where they can't reach it (your trailer tack room or in the pit toilet house). One clever raccoon managed to open our ice chest and ate a dozen eggs and a loaf of bread. The next night, he ate a whole chicken out of an ice chest in the next camp.

Facilities at the park are very rustic. Compared to those at Anza-Borrego or Chino Hills, they are downright decrepit. There is no potable water for human consumption, and the horse water is too rusty to use for human bathing or washing dishes. The horse water comes from a gravity-fed well located near Oak Camp. This presents a serious problem for those camping in

Sage or Lupine who are left completely dry if anyone below them is drawing water. Bring a rake and muck bucket or wheelbarrow to haul your horse manure to the pickup area. You must haul out your own trash. The midday sun can be quite hot. You might consider bringing a canopy because there is no shade until late afternoon.

We received significant misinformation about stabling facilities, arriving with five horses only to discover our site included two single-horse stalls, and no other stalls were available.

Here's a run-down on the facilities: **Lupine** and **Sage** each have two covered one-horse stalls. You can bring up to six horses into each of these camps, but four of them will have to be tied to your trailer or put in your own portable corrals. Each site includes a fire pit and two picnic tables; they share one pit toilet. There is one water faucet approximately 100 feet from the stalls. It might take 2 or 3 hours to fill a 10-gallon bucket. (In a pinch you can drive to Manzanita and fill your buckets there.)

Chamise and **Manzanita** each have two uncovered one-horse stalls. You can bring up to six horses into each of these camps, but four of them will have to be tied to your trailer or put in your own portable corrals. Each site includes a fire pit and two picnic tables; they share one pit toilet. There is one water faucet approximately 50 feet from the stalls. Since these camps are close to the gravity-fed well, getting water is less of a problem than in Lupine and Sage.

Reservations for Sage, Chamise, and Manzanita can be made through MISTIX up to 56 days in advance. Lupine is available on a first-come, first-served basis.

Oak and **Madrone** are for group camping and cost $60 per night. Reservations can be made through MISTIX up to 6 months in advance. Each site has four pipe corrals that can hold two horses each (three in a pinch) and six one-horse corrals. All corrals are uncovered. You may bring seven to twenty-five horses into each camp, but you'll only have corrals for a maximum of eighteen (assuming they all get along). Each camp has one pit toilet and one water faucet with good water pressure. Madrone offers a large BBQ pit.

Hot showers are available at Morro Bay State Park -- 2 minutes for twenty-five cents. (You'll be surprised what you can do with three or four quarters!) To get there take Pecho Valley Road to Los Osos Valley Road. Turn left at South Bay Boulevard. Travel 3.3 miles to Morro Bay State Park; turn left. Continue .9 miles to the entrance station. Tell the ranger you're from Montaña de Oro and he won't charge a day-use fee.

Montaña de Oro is a wonderful place to live out your childhood fantasy of riding on the beach. If you arrive prepared, your stay will be as pleasant as the sea breezes wafting up through the canyon.

Mount Piños
Chula Vista Parking Area

N

To Pine
Mtn. Club

To Frazier
Park

6800
Ft.

6200 Ft.

Chula Vista
Campground
8200 Ft.

7400
Ft.

Mt. Pinos
Hwy

7600
Ft.

7400
Ft.

Continued Below

Mc Gill
Campground

Mt. Pinos
Campground
7600 Ft.

Eastern Section

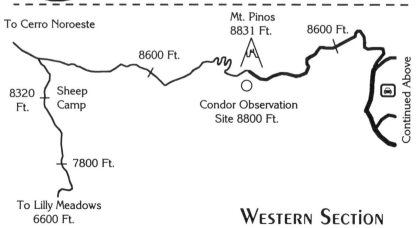

To Cerro Noroeste

Mt. Pinos
8831 Ft.

8600 Ft.

8600 Ft.

8320
Ft.

Sheep
Camp

Condor Observation
Site 8800 Ft.

Continued Above

7800 Ft.

To Lilly Meadows
6600 Ft.

Western Section

Mount Piños
Chula Vista Parking Area

Contributed by Jennifer and Rick Fuller

Located west of Frazier Park (45 miles north of the San Fernando Valley) in the Los Padres National Forest. For detailed maps and additional information, contact Mount Piños Ranger District Office, HC Box 400, 34580 Lockwood Valley Road, Frazier Park CA 93225, (805) 245-3731.

Hours	None
Fees	None
Getting There	♘ ♘ (Road closed in winter. Check conditions with ranger station.)
Parking	♘
Hitching Rails/Corrals	
Parking Area	No/No
Mount Piños Campground	No/Yes (two only)
Trail Difficulty	
Physical Ability	♘ ♘ to ♘ ♘ ♘
Training Level	♘ ♘ to ♘ ♘ ♘ ♘
Elevation	
Chula Vista Parking Area	8,200 feet
Chula Vista Parking Area to	
Condor Observation Site -- Gain	400 feet in 2 miles
Sheep Camp -- Gain	120 feet in 4.5 miles
Lilly Meadows -- Loss	-1,800 feet in 9 miles
Water	
Parking Area	People: No Horse: No
Mount Piños Campground	People: Yes Horse: Yes
Toilets	Yes, pit (bring toilet paper)
Bicyclists	Yes, 🚩 🚩 🚩 (depending on the trail)

Directions:

From Interstate 5 north of the Gorman/Hungry Valley area, exit at Frazier Park and go west 6 miles to the intersection with Lockwood Valley Road (on your left) and Lake of the Woods. Go straight ahead. You are now on Cuddy Valley Road. Continue 6 miles to the junction with Mill Potrero Road. Turn left and stay on Cuddy Valley Road 8 miles up the mountain to the large parking area at Chula Vista Campground.

Description:

After a long stretch of 100-degree summer days, you'll be ready for an escape to the cool, clean air of Mount Piños where the average summer temperature hovers around 84 degrees.

The Mount Piños area offers several scenic trails through Jeffrey pine forests and across rock-strewn ridge backs. Start by taking the dirt road 2 miles to the Mount Piños summit and condor observation site. From there, you'll have incredible views of Lockwood Valley to the south, and Pine Mountain Country Club and Bakersfield to the north.

California condors (*Gymnogyps californianus*), which number fewer than thirty, are frequently seen in flight from the observation site. With a wingspan of 9 feet, they are the largest land bird in North America. Condors may be identified in flight by the nearly straight leading edge of their wings. The adult bird has a prominent triangular patch of white under the wings and the head is orange.

From the observation site, ride west approximately 2 miles to the trail intersection. The right fork takes you to Cerro Noroeste. The left fork goes to Sheep Camp and Lilly Meadows. Lupine, paintbrush, and other wildflowers dot the landscape well into July if the previous winter rains were adequate.

Photo by Jennifer Fuller

There are no toilets, garbage cans, or water at the Chula Vista parking area. However, if you are fully self-contained, you may camp there with your horses. Remember to haul out all manure and trash so that other horse campers will be welcome.

You may also camp in the Mount Piños Campground 2 miles down the mountain from the parking area. The campground offers nineteen sites, pit toilets, and two corrals. Fires are allowed without a permit inside the campground stove. Barbecues and lanterns are okay when placed on the campsite table.

During the new moon, the Chula Vista parking area is a favorite gathering spot for amateur astronomers. You can see every type of telescope there is, and if you ask, the folks might even let you look through one.

Nicholas Flat

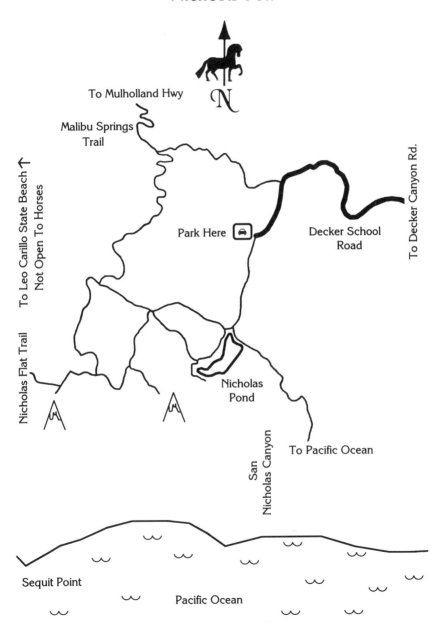

To Mulholland Hwy

Malibu Springs
Trail

N

To Leo Carillo State Beach
Not Open To Horses

Nicholas Flat Trail

Park Here

Decker School
Road

To Decker Canyon Rd.

Nicholas
Pond

San
Nicholas Canyon

To Pacific Ocean

Sequit Point

Pacific Ocean

Nicholas Flat

Located in the Leo Carrillo State Beach boundaries within the Santa Monica Mountain National Recreation Area (SMMNRA), a unit of the National Park Service, managed by the California Department of Parks and Recreation. For detailed maps and additional information, contact California Department of Parks and Recreation, 1925 Las Virgenes Rd., Calabasas CA 91302, (818) 880-0350.

Hours	None
Fee	None
Getting There	♘ ♘ ♘ ♘ **
Parking	♘ ♘ ♘ ♘
Hitching Rails/Corrals	No/No
Trail Difficulty	
Physical Ability	♘ ♘ to ♘ ♘ ♘ ♘
Training Level	♘ ♘ to ♘ ♘ ♘
Elevation Loss	
Nicholas Flat Trail	-1,700 feet in 2.5 miles
Malibu Springs Trail	-1,500 feet in 2 miles
Water	People: No Horse: Yes
Toilets	No

Directions:

Take U.S. 101 Ventura Freeway to Agoura Hills; exit at Kanan-Dume Road (N9) and turn south.   Travel 5.6 miles to Mulholland Drive and turn right (west).   Travel 1 mile to the fork in the road.   Take the left fork, which is Encinal Canyon Road. Continue 3.3 miles to Lechusa and turn right.   Travel .1 miles and turn left on Decker Road.   Travel 1.4 miles and make a hairpin right turn onto Decker School Road.   Drive to the end of the road, 1.5 miles.

** Special note about getting there and parking. We drove a Ford extended cab dually truck with a four-horse bumper-pull trailer and were just able to negotiate the hairpin turn from Decker Road onto Decker School Road. In addition, we had to make a three-point turn at the parking area to get turned around.

Description:

Nicholas Pond, sweeping ocean vistas, and easy riding on Nicholas Flat itself make this a first-rate place to explore. Untouched by fire since 1978, some of the trails are overgrown with manzanita, chaparral, and hollyleaf redberry. Be sure to check for ticks after your ride.

From the parking area, head south along a wide trail into a tree-shaded thicket -- a welcome place to stop in the heat of summer. After a short distance, the trail forks. Take the right fork. (The left fork skirts the northeast corner of Nicholas Pond and then follows the ridge between San Nicholas Canyon and Los Alisos Canyon to the ocean.) Make another left at the Nicholas Flat Trail marker and ride along the shore of Nicholas Pond. Studded with oak trees and rimmed with grasses and cat-tails, this freshwater marsh is home to many species of birds including red-winged blackbirds. Cougar, deer, coyote, and other wildlife water here, and you might encounter the Fish and Game warden checking for poachers.

According to *Wildflowers of the Santa Monica Mountains* by Milt Mc Auley, a freshwater marsh is part of the mountain's drainage system and is characterized by standing or slowly moving water. Typical plants include pond lily, watercress, and bulrushes. At the west end of the pond, follow the Nicholas Flat Trail signs west (generally to your left) and climb approximately

200 feet to the highest point of the flat, overlooking the Pacific Ocean. On a clear day, you can see the Channel Islands and as far south as Point Dume.

From the ridge, you have several options: (1)   Ride north along the Malibu Springs Trail approximately 2 miles, then take the right fork .5 miles back to Decker School Road. You'll have to ride a short distance down the road to get back to where you parked.   (2) The Malibu Springs Trail continues to Mulholland Highway, and like the Nicholas Flat Trail, is very steep and overgrown in places. (3) Or you can choose one of several interconnecting trails and circle back to Nicholas Pond.

In the spring, you'll find many wildflowers including bush monkey flower and deerweed in bloom. This is also a good place to find Catalina mariposa lily. Of the five types of mariposa lilies that grow in the Santa Monica Mountains, the Catalina -- white, tinged with lilac, with a purple spot near the base of each petal -- is the most common.

Pacific Crest Trail

The Pacific Crest National Scenic Trail (PCT) extends 2,638 miles connecting Mexico and Canada through California, Oregon, and Washington. Completed in 1993, the trail winds through desert chaparral, alpine meadows, and glaciated granite. It passes through twenty-four national forests, seven national parks, thirty-three wilderness areas, six state/province parks, and four Bureau of Land Management areas. The advocacy group for the PCT is the Pacific Crest Trail Association, a public membership association, that sponsors trail maintenance crews for the PCT and feeder trails. For more information about the Pacific Crest Trail Association, write them at 5325 Elkhorn Blvd. #256, Sacramento CA 95842, (800) 817-2243.

Although the PCT traverses several areas listed in this guide, two riding locations, Gleason Canyon (page 85) and Lone Pine Canyon (page 89), focus on PCT access. A description of Gleason Canyon and Lone Pine Canyon follows.

Pacific Crest Trail
Gleason Canyon
The Old PCT Route Through Acton

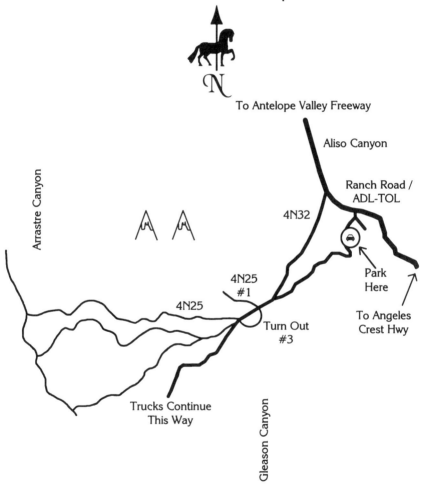

To Antelope Valley Freeway

Aliso Canyon

Ranch Road /
ADL-TOL

4N32

Arrastre Canyon

Park
Here

4N25
#1

4N25

To Angeles
Crest Hwy

Turn Out
#3

Trucks Continue
This Way

Gleason Canyon

San Gabriel Mountains

Pacific Crest Trail
Gleason Canyon
The Old PCT Route Through Acton
Angeles National Forest Route 4N25

Located southwest of the Antelope Valley in the Angeles National Forest. For detailed maps and additional information, contact Tujunga Ranger District Office, 12371 N. Little Tujunga Canyon Road, San Fernando CA 91342, (818) 899-1900.

Hours	None
Fee	None
Getting There	U U
Parking	U U
Hitching Rails/Corrals	No/No
Trail Difficulty	
Physical Ability	U U to U U U
Training Level	U to U U
Elevation Gain	100 feet in 3 miles. Start at 3,200 feet.
Water	People: No Horse: Seasonal
Toilets	No

Directions:

Take the 14 Antelope Valley Freeway to Acton; exit at Santiago Road and turn south. After 1 mile, Santiago Road ends at Soledad Canyon Road. Turn right (west) onto Soledad Canyon. Travel .5 miles and turn left (south) onto Aliso Canyon Road. Travel 3 miles, cross an old white wooden bridge, and then turn right on Ranch Road. This is an Edison/Department of Water & Power (DWP) easement and you'll see their sign "ADL-TOL." Fifty yards in, the road splits. Take the right fork and drive toward the large metal power pole. Keep to the right and circle around this pole, parking where you meet the road again. This allows plenty of room for other visitors to park behind you.

Description:

The trail follows dirt road easements for the Edison/DWP power poles that traverse this area and national forest roads. Gently sloping and well cleared, the trails are wide enough to ride two abreast, making this a nice family riding location. The Pacific Crest Trail used to cut through Gleason Canyon over to Arrastre Canyon, and you can still see and ride on parts of it.

From the parking area, ride west along the Edison/DWP easement. You'll drop down into Gleason Canyon and cross a seasonal creek, headwater of the Santa Clara River. Climbing out of the creek bed, you'll ride generally west through pristine high desert. Manzanita, sage, and chaparral predominate, joined by a profusion of wildflowers each spring. One-half mile up, you'll connect with Angeles Forest Route 4N32 (no signpost). This route is heavily used by tractor-trailer rigs carrying ore from a private mine up the canyon, so keep an ear tuned for the sound of trucks and be ready to ride off the road until they pass. Continue less than .25 miles until you come to "Turnout #3" on your left. On your right will be Forest Route Marker 4N25. Ignore this and stay on 4N32 a bit further until you come to the other end of "Turnout #3." On your right is a dirt track leading toward the power lines. This is also Route 4N25 and a good place to start a 5-mile loop ride. Just beyond this intersection, 4N32 (the truck route) forks, and the trucks turn left, leaving plenty of trails for peaceful riding through the saddle between Gleason and Arrastre Canyons.

The loop trail takes you along the hills between Gleason and Arrastre Canyons, giving excellent views, and in the spring, an explosion of wildflowers including poppies, sandwort, fiddleneck, broom, paintbrush, buckwheat, and chia. A few hundred yards downhill and to your left is another Edison/DWP access road -- the return portion of the loop. As you ride, you'll notice other trails crossing Arrastre Canyon offering plenty of opportunities to explore.

Only a few minutes by car from downtown Acton, Gleason Canyon is peaceful and uncrowded -- a most enjoyable place for you and your family to spend a few hours.

One final note: After a hot summer ride, check out the real ice cream milk shakes made by E-Z Take-out Burger at the corner of the Antelope Valley Freeway and Santiago Road. They make great burgers and fries, too, for a very reasonable price.

Pacific Crest Trail
Lone Pine Canyon

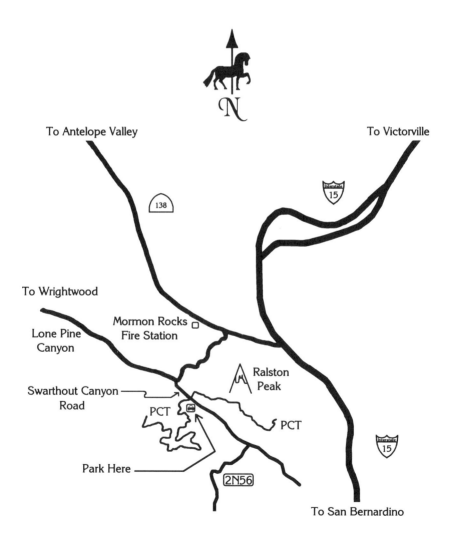

Pacific Crest Trail
Lone Pine Canyon

Located west of the Cajon Pass in the San Bernardino National Forest. For detailed maps and additional information, contact Cajon Ranger District Office, Star Route, Box 100, 1209 Lytle Creek Rd., Fontana CA 92336-9704, (909) 794-1123.

Hours	None
Fee	None
Getting There	♘ ♘
Parking	♘ ♘ ♘
Hitching Rails/Corrals	No/No
Trail Difficulty	
Physical Ability	♘ ♘ ♘ to ♘ ♘ ♘ ♘
Training Level	♘ ♘ ♘ to ♘ ♘ ♘ ♘
Elevation Gain	Depends on route and distance. Start at 3,600 ft.
Water	People: No Horse: No
Toilets	No

Directions:

From the San Fernando/Santa Clarita Valley area: Take the 14 Antelope Valley Freeway north and exit at Pearblossom Highway. Go northeast 5 miles to Four Points. Turn right and continue on 138 Pearblossom Highway for 38 miles to Mormon Rocks. Just past the Mormon Rocks Ranger/Fire Station, turn right on Lone Pine Canyon Road.

From the San Bernardino area: Take Interstate 15 north to Cajon Junction. Exit at 138 Pearblossom Highway and go west. Travel 1.3 miles to Lone Pine Canyon Road; turn left. If you pass the Mormon Rocks Ranger/Fire Station, you've gone too far.

Both: After 1.5 miles, Lone Pine Canyon Road curves sharply to the right and just as you come out of the curve you'll see Swarthout Canyon Road on your left. Turn left here. Travel .5 miles, **watching carefully** for a small dirt road on your right. Turn right for a few yards, then back into the parking area. (There's room for three or four four-horse rigs.) If you miss this parking area, continue 2 miles down Swarthout Canyon Road until the junction of 2N56 where you can turn around.

Description:

Access to the PCT here offers splendid opportunities for the horse and rider looking for a challenge.   If you aren't that adventurous or as well conditioned, you can make a short loop ride on the PCT, then explore north and south along old dirt roads in the belly of Lone Pine Canyon.

To access PCT: If you were sharp-eyed when driving in, you noticed PCT signposts on either side of Swarthout Canyon Road approximately 50 yards north of the parking area. (Don't worry if you missed them. They are much easier to see if you pass the parking area altogether and have to turn around and come back!) Another way to access the PCT is to take the dirt road due west from the parking area for about .25 miles where you'll come to a concrete water tank. Just past this water tank, the PCT crosses the dirt trail. If you go left, you'll climb through dense chaparral along Upper Lytle Creek Ridge. The trail here is narrow and steep and, with ceanothus and chamise crowding the path, an excellent place to pick up ticks.

If you turn right past the water tank, you'll circle back toward the parking area and eventually cross Swarthout Canyon Road. This makes a nice, but short, loop for the less-conditioned rider. East of Swarthout Canyon, the PCT circles Ralston Peak and eventually crosses Interstate 15 further east.   Take only well-conditioned and experienced horses along the shoulder of Ralston Peak as the trail is steep, narrow, and soft with no place to turn around.

During the spring, wildflowers and beaver-tail cactus color the landscape.   In May, the yuccas send up their creamy white flower stalks.   Spring comes later here because of the higher elevation. When most of the flowers are done at the lower elevations, you'll still find good flower viewing here.

Reyes Creek Campground
Piedra Blanca National Recreation Trail

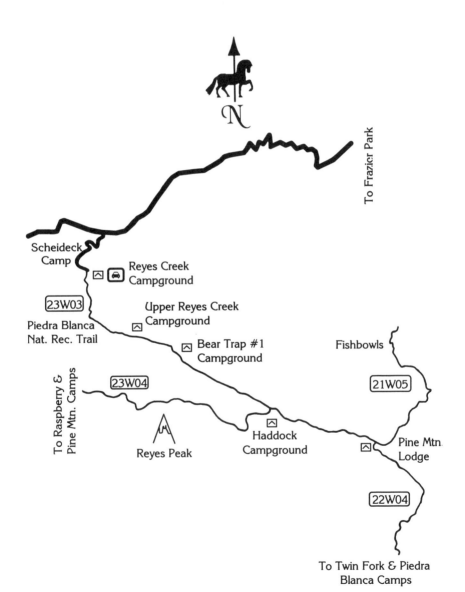

Reyes Creek Campground
Piedra Blanca National Recreation Trail

Contributed by Jennifer and Rick Fuller

Located west of Frazier Park in the Los Padres National Forest. For detailed maps and additional information, contact Mount Piños Ranger District Office, HC 1 Box 400, 34580 Lockwood Valley Road, Frazier Park CA 93225, (805) 245-3731.

Hours
  Day Use .... None
  Overnight .... None
Fees
  Day Use .... None
  Overnight .... $5/night (first-come, first-served)
Getting There .... 𝖀 𝖀 𝖀 𝖀 **
Parking .... 𝖀 𝖀
Hitching Rails/Corrals
  Day Use .... No/Yes, if available
  Overnight .... No/Yes. Two 20-by-20-foot corrals are available for all equestrian campers. You may tie to your trailer or bring portable stalls.
Trail Difficulty
  Physical Ability .... 𝖀 𝖀 to 𝖀 𝖀 𝖀 𝖀
  Training Level .... 𝖀 𝖀 𝖀 to 𝖀 𝖀 𝖀 𝖀
Elevation Gain .... Depends on route and distance. Start at 4,000 feet.
  Staging to Upper Reyes .... 700 feet in 3 miles
  Staging to Bear Trap #1 .... 1,000 feet in 5 miles
  Staging to Haddock & Jct.
    with trail 23W04 .... 2,080 feet in 8 miles
Water .... *People: No* Horse: Yes, creek and water trough
Toilets .... Yes, pit

Directions:

From Los Angeles: Take Interstate 5 north to the Frazier Park exit; turn left (west). (From Bakersfield: Take Interstate 5 south to Frazier Park; exit and turn right.) Travel 6.5 miles to Lockwood Valley Road and turn left. Continue 27 miles on Lockwood Valley Road watching for the brown Reyes Creek Campground/Piedra Blanca Trail sign (National Forest Route 7N11); turn left. Continue 1.5 miles through Schiedick Camp until you enter Reyes Creek Campground. Follow the one-way road through the campground to the sign that reads "Trailhead." Turn here and go over a fairly steep hill to the equestrian parking area.

** Note: The 1.5-mile road through Schiedick Camp is very narrow and winding. We wouldn't recommend anything longer than a 21-foot gooseneck trailer and crew-cab combo. The last corner before reaching the campground is very tight.

Description:

If you missed the spring wildflower show in the Santa Monica Mountains, Anza-Borrego, or Chino Hills, consider this day ride from Reyes Creek Campground. Starting at the 4,000-foot elevation and climbing to 6,080 feet at Haddock camp, you'll see plenty of bloom well into June and, perhaps, July.

A potpourri of sugar pine and sage sweetens the air as you begin your ride from the equestrian parking area at the well-marked Piedra Blanca trailhead. Overhead, a red-tailed hawk circles lazily against the sparkling azure sky. The trail is quiet, except for the steady hum of insects, the muffled clop of your horse's hooves, and the creak of your saddle. You'll traverse barren outcroppings where the hot sun sends beads of sweat down your back, splash through bubbling Reyes Creek, and amble through cool, tree-shaded thickets. On a hot summer day, the Piedra Blanca National Recreation Trail is the place to ride.

The trail is well marked, although it shrinks to approximately 2 feet wide in places. If winter rains are substantial and you ride early in the season, chaparral may have overtaken portions of the trail. Check trail conditions with the Mount Piños Ranger Station before starting out.

Photo by Jennifer Fuller

Because there are many hikers, we chose to remove the manure our horses so kindly left. If you keep a good humor, it's no big deal to dismount and remove it. (We may have discovered a new version of golf!)

Be sure to pack and use a good equine fly repellent. A wet winter and spring will produce a very successful mosquito crop. For your own comfort, bring the citronella candles and some bug repellent for yourself.

Reyes Creek Campground offers thirty overnight sites for equestrian campers, and sites are usually available on non-holiday weekends. The equestrian parking area is 300 to 400 yards from the campground, which may bother those folks who like to camp within sight of their animals. If you are self-contained, you can set up camp in the equestrian parking area; otherwise, choose a site in the campground. Water from Reyes Creek and a trough at the parking area are available for your horses. Creek water is not recommended for human consumption unless purified. To be safe, bring drinking water from home. Each campsite offers a table and stove. Eight pit toilets and several garbage cans are located throughout the campground. Fire wood permits are for sale year-round. Call the Mount Piños Ranger Station for more information. And please remember to bring whatever tools you need to clean up after your horses.

Although the campground is open year-round, it does receive winter snow. If you plan to ride in the late fall, winter, or early spring, check weather conditions with the ranger station before leaving home.

"WHEN I AM WITH A HORSE,

WE GO TOGETHER.

WE GO AS A TEAM,

WITH A LEADER AND A FOLLOWER,

like DANCE PARTNERS."

Jennifer Ormerod
Crown Valley Horsemanship Center
Acton, CA

Rocky Peak Park

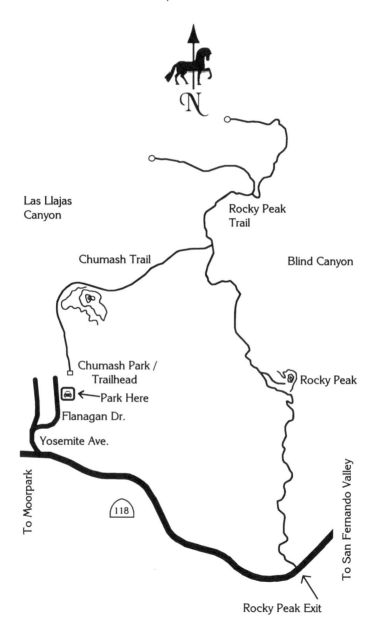

N

Las Llajas
Canyon

Rocky Peak
Trail

Chumash Trail

Blind Canyon

Chumash Park /
Trailhead

Rocky Peak

Park Here

Flanagan Dr.

Yosemite Ave.

To Moorpark

118

To San Fernando Valley

Rocky Peak Exit

Rocky Peak Park
Chumash Trail and Rocky Peak Trail

Located in east Simi Valley. For detailed maps and additional information, contact Rancho Simi Recreation and Park District Office, 2900 Royal Ave., Simi Valley CA 93065, (805) 255-0640.

Hours	None
Fee	None
Getting There	U
Parking	U U (Bring a shovel to pick up manure. You'll be parking on a residential street.)
Hitching Rails/Corrals	No/No
Trail Difficulty	
Physical Ability	U U to U U U U
Training Level	U U to U U U U
Elevation Gain	
Chumash Trail	1,060 feet in 2.5 miles
Rocky Peak Trail	1,040 feet in 6.5 miles
Water	People: No Horse: No
Toilets	No
Bicyclists	Yes, 🏁 🏁 🏁

Directions:

Take the 118 Ronald Reagan Freeway (formerly the Simi Valley Freeway) to Simi Valley, exit at Yosemite, and go north. Travel .5 miles to Flanagan Drive and turn right. Go .8 miles to the end of Flanagan Drive. Park on the street. Rocky Peak Park is ahead and on your right. To avoid a three-point turnaround when you leave, make a left on Mescallero, then left on Calusa, then left on Mohican, and finally, a right on Flanagan (you are now heading back to Yosemite).

Description:

Rocky Peak Park, 4,369 acres of rolling grasslands, dramatic sandstone outcroppings, and steep cliffs, straddles Ventura and Los Angeles Counties in the Santa Susana Mountains. It includes Las Llajas Canyon, Blind Canyon, and the famous Rocky Peak. If you and your horse are well conditioned and have a "helper" who can move your rig, you can make a 9-mile "reverse" ride starting at the Rocky Peak overpass to the 118 Ronald Reagan Freeway and ending at the park entrance on Flanagan Drive (it's less steep this way).

The two main trails in the park are the Rocky Peak Trail, running roughly north and south, and the Chumash Trail, which intersects it. Both trails are steep and very narrow (2 feet or less) in areas. Bring a hat, sunscreen lotion, and plenty of water for both you and your horse.

The area is frequented by mountain bicyclists, and where the trails are narrow, this can be a major problem. Usually, when encountering a bicyclist on the trail, the cyclist should stop, stand to the outside trail edge, continue talking, and wait quietly for the horseback rider to pass. With the trails at Rocky Peak so narrow, we found it easier (and safer) to snuggle our horses up against the mountainside while the cyclists dismounted and carried their bikes past us (hanging out over the canyon).

If your horse is not "bomb proof" enough for an encounter like this, you'll still be able to enjoy the area. Consider a short, 1.5-mile ride up the Chumash Trail, stopping before it gets narrow. You'll have great views of Simi Valley. (If you ride to the top you can see the Pacific Ocean and Anacapa Island, too.) Then return to the trailhead and ride northwest across the grasslands toward Las Llajas Canyon. The area was once part of the vast Runkle Ranch property and you may encounter range cattle. In Las Llajas Canyon you'll find a beautiful seasonal creek lined with cottonwood trees and cattails. You can also ride south and east from the trailhead in the foothills north of State Highway 118.

Deer, coyote, fox, badger, bobcat, and rattlesnakes make their home in the park. In the most remote areas you might see black bear and mountain lion. The park is part of a protected wildlife corridor that allows animals to travel between the Santa Susana and Santa Monica Mountains. The park contains many wildflowers, sage, grasses, and a few oak trees. Spring is the best time for wildflower viewing.

Sawmill Mountain

N

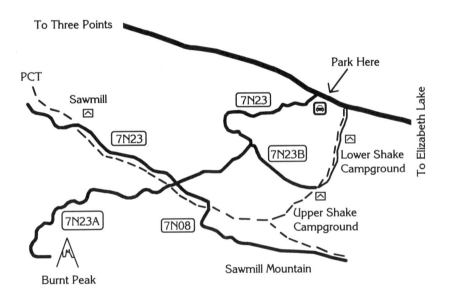

To Three Points

Park Here

PCT

Sawmill

7N23

To Elizabeth Lake

7N23

7N23B

Lower Shake
Campground

Upper Shake
Campground

7N23A

7N08

Burnt Peak

Sawmill Mountain

Sawtooth Mtn

Sawmill Mountain

Located east of Gorman (40 miles north of the San Fernando Valley) in the Angeles National Forest. For detailed maps and additional information, contact Saugus District Office, 30800 Bouquet Canyon Road, Saugus CA 91350, (805) 252-9710.

Hours .... None
Fee .... None
Getting There .... U
Parking .... U U
Hitching Rails/Corrals .... No/No
Trail Difficulty
    Physical Ability .... U U U to U U U U
    Training Level .... U U
Elevation Gain
    From Parking to Jct. with 7N34 .... 900 feet in 2 miles
    From Parking to Jct. with 7N08 .... 1,300 feet in 3 miles
    From Parking to Sawmill Camp .... 1,700 feet in 5 miles
    From Parking to Burnt Peak .... 2,000 feet in 7 miles
Water .... People: No Horse: No
Toilets .... Yes, pit at Lower Shake
    Campground
Off-Road Vehicles .... Yes,

Directions:

From Antelope Valley: Exit the 14 Antelope Valley Freeway at Palmdale Boulevard and go west. Travel 16 miles (through Leona Valley) until you come to a "T" intersection with Elizabeth Lake Road. Turn left onto Elizabeth Lake Road. Drive 9.5 miles. Watch for the Forest Service sign on your left that reads "Upper Shake -- 3 miles, Sawmill -- 5 miles, Burnt Peak -- 7 miles." Park here.

From I-5: Take Interstate 5 to the Gorman/Hungry Valley area; exit at State Highway 138/Palmdale-Lancaster. Go east on State Highway 138 for 13.2 miles to Three Points Road; turn right (south). Travel 3 miles to Three Points; veer left (east) onto Pine Canyon Road. Travel 5 miles. Watch for the brown Forest Service sign on your right that reads "Upper Shake -- 3 miles, Sawmill -- 5 miles, Burnt Peak -- 7 miles." Park here.

Description:

From the parking area, head up Forest Route 7N23, a wide dirt road flanked by a mixture of oaks, pine, and cedar. You'll

Photo by Paulette Mouchet

climb steadily on this leg, but the views are worth it: sweeping vistas of Holiday Valley and the Tehachapi Mountains to the north, and during poppy season, great swaths of orange, purple, and yellow flowers on the Antelope Valley floor.   You may encounter a vehicle or two along the way, but there's room to pass comfortably.

After approximately 2 miles, you'll come to the first junction. On your left is 7N23B (also known as 7N34), which takes you to Upper and Lower Shake Campgrounds through Shake Canyon. A perennial stream bubbles alongside the trail, nourishing a variety of flowers and shade trees.   On the downside, insects can be a problem.   Be sure to use a strong repellent on your horse and carry something for yourself in case the bugs get too pesky. The trail is quite narrow in places, but if you have a confident, sure-footed horse, it's a beautiful ride.

From this first junction, you can continue another mile up 7N23 to the second junction that provides great views of Burnt Peak and the National Forest.   Red paintbrush, pink and white buckwheat, elderberry, and lupine all thrive here, offering a show of flowers in the spring and summer.

At this second junction, you have three riding options. Straight ahead is the trail to Burnt Peak, 4 miles away, which may or may not be open.   To your right, 7N23 continues to Sawmill Campground.   To your left is 7N08, which follows the ridge of Sawmill Mountain east toward Lake Hughes.   The last mile of this trail zigzags from the ridge top down to Elizabeth Lake Road at Lake Hughes.   The Pacific Crest Trail also crosses through this second junction, but it's quite narrow for riding.

As you pause on Sawmill Mountain ridge overlooking row after row of untamed mountains, it's hard to believe a place like this exists so close to civilization.   With the wide trails, this area is a nice place to bring the whole family.

Vasquez Rocks County Park

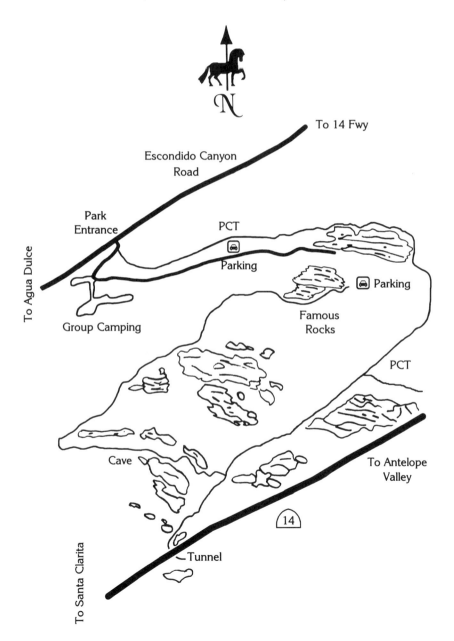

Vasquez Rocks County Park

A 745-acre park located southwest of the Antelope Valley in the foothills between the San Gabriel and Sierra Pelona Mountains. Address: 10700 W. Escondido Canyon Road, Agua Dulce CA 91350, (805) 268-0840.

Hours .... 8 A.M. to Sunset. Overnight stays for groups only, by special arrangement.

Fee .... $3 per vehicle (exact change required)

Getting There .... ♘

Parking .... ♘

Hitching Rails/Corrals .... No/No

Trail Difficulty

    Physical Ability .... ♘ ♘ to ♘ ♘ ♘ ♘

    Training Level .... ♘ ♘ to ♘ ♘ ♘ ♘

Elevation Gain .... Depends on route and distance. Start at 2,800 ft.

Water .... People: Yes Horse: Yes

Toilets .... Yes, flush and pit

Directions:

Take the 14 Antelope Valley Freeway to Agua Dulce, exit at Agua Dulce Canyon Road, and go north. Travel approximately 2 miles until you reach a stop sign. Continue straight ahead. You are now on Escondido Canyon Road. Travel approximately .3 miles beyond the stop sign. Park entrance is on your right.

Description:

The distinctive sandstone rock formations were shelter for the Tataviam Indians, a hideout for the infamous bandit Tiburcio Vasquez, and became Bedrock City for *The Flinstones* movie. You've seen them in Taco Bell commercials, the original *Star Trek* series, and dozens of old westerns.

Riding along dry streambeds, through rugged gullies, and over sandstone fingers jutting out at odd angles, it's easy to see how Vasquez eluded the law here. You never quite know what awaits you over the next rise. Make your ride as easy or difficult as you like by sticking to obvious trails or taking an adventurous cross-country approach. No worries about getting lost: the landmark rock formations are easily visible from most locations. For the well-seasoned horse and rider, check out the Pacific Crest Trail, which passes through the park.

East of the entrance to the group camping area is a short interpretative trail with markers identifying native plants. Yucca cacti, sometimes called Our Lord's Candle, bloom in May and the stems, covered with cream-colored flowers, are spectacular to see near sundown. This is rattlesnake and mountain lion country (see precautions listed on page 13), although on a recent August ride, the author saw none.

Spring may be the best time of the year for a visit when wildflowers paint the landscape and seasonal streams are running. Summer is hot. Bring a hat, sunscreen, and plenty of water. Horse water troughs are located approximately 1,000 feet east of the end of the main park road. Picnic tables may be found throughout the park, some shaded, and you'll find a soda machine and pay phone near the park office. There's plenty of parking and space to turn your rig around without backing up.

Whether geological, archaeological, or celluloid, you'll enjoy a piece of history when you ride in Vasquez County Park.

GENERAL EQUIPMENT AND SUPPLIES

- Wear protective clothing including gloves, hat, and sturdy boots or riding tennis shoes. Protective head gear is available in western hat styles. See page 118 for sources.
- Sunglasses, sunscreen, insect repellent, and lip protection. A bandanna will keep the sun off your neck.
- Water. Allow 1 gallon per person per day. Allow at least 10 gallons per horse. You can purchase collapsible 5-gallon containers from a camping or sporting goods store.
- A map of the area and this guidebook
- Pocket knife
- Wire cutters
- Hook pick (carry in saddlebags)
- First-aid kit for both horse and rider
- Spare halter and lead rope
- Buckets for water. Consider carrying a folding bucket in your saddlebag to use when water is available but not convenient to approach with your horse.
- Pen and paper
- Leather thong (for mending tack and tying things)
- Fire extinguisher
- Paper towels, wet wipes
- Flashlight (with spare batteries and bulb)
- Trash bag
- Folding chairs
- Waterproof matches (first-aid kit is a good place to store them)
- Manure rake
- Camera

FIRST-AID KIT

From *Mountaineering First Aid*, first aid is defined as "the immediate care given to a person who has been injured or suddenly taken ill." This means first aid must be started in a relatively short time, even though evacuation may be delayed. This includes not only care of physical injuries and protection from the environment, but also care for the victim's mental well-being.

Unless you are dealing with severe, unstoppable blood loss, poisonous bites (snake, spider, scorpion), severe allergic reaction (bee sting), or heart attack, most accidents are not immediately life-threatening. Your goal in giving first aid is to stabilize the patient (horse or human) for transport to a medical facility. With this in mind, we suggest the following first-aid kit:

- Emergency first-aid book for both horse and human. **Read and re-read these books ahead of time. First aid requires a cool head and a plan of action.**
- 3 rolls of Vetrap or other cohesive flexible bandage
- 2 rolls of 4-inch-wide Elastikon or other flexible adhesive bandaging tape
- 3–6 individually wrapped unscented, unpowdered sanitary napkins (absorbent wound dressing)
- 3 rolls brown gauze
- Safety pins
- Pen and paper
- Scissors
- Duct tape
- Easyboot
- Hydrogen peroxide and/or Betadine solution

- 1 extra-large syringe (for irrigating wounds)
- Coins for pay telephone
- Hemostat
- Snake bite antivenin and/or Sawyer Extractor. (Contact your doctor and veterinarian for recommendation.)
- 2 pieces of rubber hosing 3 to 4 inches long (to keep nostrils from swelling shut in case of snake bite)
- Thermometer. If you purchase plastic sheaths, you can use the same thermometer for both horse and human.
- 2–3 rolls of 4-inch-wide bandaging gauze
- Sterile adhesive bandages 1-by-3 inches and other assorted sizes (at least 6)
- 10 sterile butterfly closures, small and large
- Tweezers
- Alcohol prep swabs
- Instant cold pack
- Disposable cloths such as Handi Wipes
- Eye wash
- 2 tubes noncortisone eye ointment
- 10 4-by-4-inch sterile gauze pads
- Antiseptic/antibiotic cream, lotion, or liquid
- Compact emergency blanket
- Moleskin and Molefoam
- Antihistamines for human
- Dipyrone (for spasmodic colic, muscular strain)
- Banamine paste (for muscle disorders, lameness, or colic)
- 1 bottle dexamethosone (for allergic reactions, swelling, and fever)
- 1 small bottle acepromazine (tranquilizer)
- Assorted needles and syringes
- Phenylbutazone paste or tablets (for muscle inflammation and lameness)
- Human pain reliever such as aspirin

ON-THE-ROAD SOURCES
FOR LOCAL VETERINARIANS

"The Equine Connection" sponsored by the American Association of Equine Practitioners is a database of member veterinarians. If you are riding during the week and need an emergency veterinarian, give them a call at (800) 438-2386. The line is staffed Monday through Friday 8:00 A.M. to 6:00 P.M., central time.

The *North American Horse Travel Guide* lists veterinarians and farriers across the United States and Canada. To order a copy, call (800) 366-0600, or write Roundup Press, P.O. Box 109, Boulder CO 80306-0109.

GENERAL INFORMATION SOURCES

American Horse Council
   1700 K Street NW
   Washington DC 20006
   (202) 296-4031

Backcountry Horsemen of California, Inc.
   P.O. Box 520
   Springville CA 93265
   (209) 539-3394

Equestrian Trails, Inc.
   13741 Foothill Blvd. #220
   Sylmar CA 91342
   (818) 362-6819

MISTIX State Park Reservation System
   P.O. Box 85705
   San Diego CA 92138-5705
   (800) 444-7275

National Forest Reservation Center
   (800) 280-2267
   Monday through Friday 8:30 A.M. to 10:30 P.M.
   Saturday and Sunday 11:00 A.M. to 7:00 P.M.

North American Trail Ride Conference
   P.O. Box 338
   Sedalia CO 80135-0338
   (719) 481-8829

Protective Head Gear
    International Riding Helmets
        205 Industrial Loop
        Staten Island, NY 10309
        (800) 435-6380
    Lexington Safety Products
        480 Fairman Rd.
        Lexington KY 40511
        (606) 233-1404
    State Line Tack
        Route 121
        P.O. Box 1217
        Plaistow NH 03865-1217
        (800) 228-9208

Stabling Directory and Equestrian Vacation Guide
    Equine Travelers of America, Inc.
    P.O. Box NR-322
    Arkansas City KS 67005-0332
    (316) 442-8131

U.S.G.S. (U.S. Department of the Interior,
    U.S. Geological Survey)
    Earth Science Information Center
    345 Middlefield Road, MS-532
    Menlo Park CA 94025-3591
    (415) 329-4309, fax (415) 329-5130

BIBLIOGRAPHY

American Horse Council. *1994 Horse Industry Directory*. Washington, D.C.: American Horse Council, 1994.

Douglass, Don and Delaine Fragnoli, ed. *Mountain Biking Southern California's Best 100 Trails*. Bishop, Calif.: Fine Edge Productions, 1993.

Equus magazine. Various issues.

Hogan, Elizabeth L., ed. *Sunset Western Garden Book*. Menlo Park, Calif.: Lane Publishing Co., 1988.

Lancaster Woman's Club. *Antelope Valley Wildflower Guide*. Lancaster, Calif.: Saint Raphael Press, 1978.

Lentz, Martha J., Ph.D., R.N., Steven C. Macdonald, M.P.H., E.M.T., and Jan D. Carline, Ph.D. *Mountaineering First Aid: A Guide to Accident Response and First Aid Care*. 3d ed., rev. Seattle, Wash.: The Mountaineers, 1990.

Life Nature Library. *The Desert*. New York: Time-Life Books, 1962.

Lindsay, Lowell and Diana Lindsay. *The Anza-Borrego Desert Region: A Guide to the State Park and Adjacent Areas*. Berkeley, Calif.: Wilderness Press, 1991.

Mc Auley, Milt. *Wildflowers of the Santa Monica Mountains*. Canoga Park, Calif.: Canyon Publishing Co., 1985.

Robinson, John W. *San Bernardino Mountain Trails: 100 Hikes in Southern California*. Berkeley, Calif: Wilderness Press, 1986.

_____ . *Trails of the Angeles: 100 Hikes in the San Gabriels.* Berkeley, Calif.: Wilderness Press, 1993.

Southern & Central California Atlas & Gazetteer. Freeport, Maine: DeLorme Mapping, 1990.

Western Horseman magazine. Various issues.

Williamson, Joseph F., ed. *Sunset Western Garden Book.* Menlo Park, Calif.: Lane Publishing Company, 1995.

INDEX

A

B

C

D

M

N

O

P

Q

R

CROWN VALLEY PRESS
P.O. Box 336 ◆ Acton, CA 93510
(805) 269-1525

To order additional copies of
Horseback Riding Trails of Southern California
use this form (or a facsimile):

	Quantity	Extension
Horseback Riding Trails of Southern California, **Volume I** $14.95 --------------------------------	_____	$_____
Horseback Riding Trails of Southern California, **Volume II** (avail. 11/15/96, call for price) ---	_____	$_____

Subtotal-- $_____

Tax 8.25% -- $_____

Handling/Shipping (add $3.00 for the first book,
$1.50 for each additional book) -------------------------- $_____

TOTAL -- $_____

Prices subject to change.
Please include a check or money order for the total.

THANK YOU FOR YOUR ORDER!

Do You Know A Great Trail?
Would You Like To Contribute To The Next Volume?

Please fill out the form below (or a facsimile) and mail to Crown Valley Press, P.O. Box 336, Acton CA 93510. Paulette Mouchet will review all submissions and notify you if your trail(s) has been selected.

Name _____

Address _____

City_____ State _____

Phone_____ Fax_____

Where is the trail located? If you have brochures or maps, please send a copy.

Using the legend on page 19 of this book, rate:
    Getting There   Parking

Are there overnight facilities? If so, please describe them including fees, corrals, water, etc. (Attach a separate sheet if necessary.)

Please indicate:

    Hours of Operation

    Fees   Toilets (pit, flush)

    Hitching Rails   Corrals

    Horse Water   People Water

Have you encountered off-road vehicles or bicyclists? If so, please use the legend on page 19 to rate the trail.

(over)

Describe the trail footing. Is it flat, steep, rocky, sandy? Are there water crossings, bridges, or other obstacles?

Using the legend on page 19, please rate the trail for:
    Physical Ability   Training Level

What makes this trail special? (Attach a separate sheet if necessary.)

Do you have photos available?